Contents

Apple Watch Series 5 for the Elderly

A Newbie to Expert Guide with Tips and Tricks to Master the New Apple Watch Series 5 in the New WatchOS 06 and ECG APP for the Elderly

NELSON NEWMAN

Introduction

Congratulations on buying your new Apple Watch Series 5. You deserve to get the best experience out of you new topnotch device. If you have just bought the new Apple Watch series 5, we have got the right tips that you need to know about your brand new device so you can familiarize yourself with the brilliant Apple Watch series 5, and learn lots of tips and tricks to do amazing things.

In case you do not know, the Apple Watch series 5 now offers more powerful, modern, and fun ways to use the watch as an extension of an iPhone. This bad boy is designed from the inside out to do a lot of innovative things you could ever imagine.

Apart from the fact that it now flaunts a bigger screen, thinner body in the same size watch casing, you can now use it to check your heart rate, lose weight, monitor your workout, and shop with it, using Apple Pay.

You can even make calls with it, use the fall detection feature to call for help if you fall and keep track of your heart rate with the new ECG App.

Did I also mention that you can use it with your Airpods? Yes you can.

What is new in the WatchOS 6

The WatchOS 6 is the latest version of the operating system that has been designed to run on the **Apple Watch Series 5.**

The watchOS 6 now offers new features such as:

• A new dedicated App Store

• An enabled Siri

• Updated apps

• A new watch face

• New health features

• And A lot more

APP STORE

Get more Apps on Apple Watch from Apple Store

Apple has designed a new App store you can easily access on your wrist through the new watchOS 6 unlike in previous operating systems were you will have to get on your iPhone before you can get apps downloaded.

The new watchOS 6 now gives you the flexibility to get Apps downloaded directly on the App store on your watch without having to use your iPhone.

This new featured App Store enables you to search for Apps or make use of the Siri voice assistance to get your searches done.

The App Store also allows you to get Apps installed on the watch as soon as they are downloaded. The watchOS 6 app store also provides different product pages for your Apps from which you can check to get the needed information about each app.

Any app can easily be purchased; downloaded and installed directly from the product page as well. And you will see information such as:

- Reviews

- App details

- Screenshots

- Ratings

- And many more

Apple has also designed some pre-installed apps to work with your watchOS 6 App stores to give you the flexibility to delete a large number of pre-installed watchOS 6 apps. Apps such as Stopwatch, Camera Remote, Radion, ECG, Walkie-talkie, Noise, Cycle tracks, etc, are apps that can be deleted. They have also been able to add a new Noise app that is designed to measure the environment's noise level and notify you against loud sounds that can cause damage to your ears.

Once the decibel level gets to 90 decibels, you will be automatically notified. (See Chapter 7 for Apps on Apple Watch)

The Always On Display

The series 5 introduced the Always on Display feature, which enables you to see the clock always. You can also adjust the refresh rate of the display from 60 hz down to 1 hz when you're not using it.

This will help the Smartwatch save a ton of battery life. (For more info, see Chapter 4— **Always On Display)**

Audiobooks

Apple has integrated a new Audiobooks app which enables you to listen to audiobooks directly from the watch on your wrist unlike before when you will need to start the audiobook on your iPhone before getting access.

The titles of your Apple books that are available on your **Reading Now** list will automatically get synced to your watch.

To play your Audiobook, all you need to do is to tap on the book cover in the Audiobook app and the Audiobook will start to play where you stopped before irrespective of the device you were using to listen.(See Chapter 33—Listen To Audiobooks)

Calculator

The new watchOS 6 also has the calculator added to it which enables you to get calculations done on time directly from your Apple watch. The calculator is made up of a built-in tool that enables you to calculate and split bills with friends.

(See Chapter 19—Use Calculator on Apple Watch)

Voice Memos

The Voice memos have also been added to the Apple watch through its new watchOS 6, which now lets you get voice-based notes recorded quickly. You can also get your thoughts recorded with a quick press on the watch face of the Apple watch on your wrist. (Chapter 34—Voice Memos)

Reminders

Just like in the Reminders app available in the iOS 13 and macOS Catalina, the new watchOS 6 also has its Reminders app updated as well. With the new interface right on the Apple watch on your wrist, the Reminders enables you to get a new reminder scheduled more quickly.

By scrolling with a finger or using the digital crown, you will get quick access to all the different sections such as Flagged, today, scheduled and all categories as well as individual lists of reminders categories that you must have created.

Messages

The new Animoji stickers are now supported by the messages through the new watchOS 6. This enables you to send your personalized stickers including the Memoji stickers though it should be noted that this will work only if the Memoji stickers are in the recently sent character list ported from the new iPhone.

(See Chapter 29: How to Read and Reply Messages on Apple Watch)

New Watch Faces

The new Numerals Duo and Numerals Mono faces have been introduced through the watchOS, with both focusing on placing the time at the center and front.

The Numerals Duo displays the time in a digital readout form while the Numerals Mono displays the hour in a digital format as well as providing an analog face.

The new watch faces that were introduced by Apple through its new watchOS are

Modular compact, the solar dial, Gradient, California, Numerals Mono and Numerals Duo with each of these faces having a unique look.

Note that some of these faces are only limited to the latest Apple watches.

There is also a new Modular compact watch face feature which is similar to the standard Modular face.

As the name suggests, it's able to have more complications fitted in, unlike the original Modular face.

It provides you with a large watch face dial alongside complications.

With the Gradient watch face, you can now select a color and it animates as time passes then helping with the shift of the gradient location.

The Solar dial feature of the watch face visualized the sun in a 24-hour path manner around the dial by shifting through the day and night continually.

The California watch face provides a standard analog dial and it is also made up of a unique mix of standard numbers with Roman numerals used in updating you about the time. (See Chapter 15: Apple Watch Faces and their Features)

Activity Trends

The new watchOS 6 is made up of Activity trends that can be viewed on the iPhone as well. The Activity trends help in comparing the progress you have made over the last 90 days to the progress made before 365 days to monitor the improvement in your trends.

In a situation where your activity levels are declining instead of trending in an upward manner, the activity trend will provide health tips to keep you motivated.

Trending upwards or downwards is denoted by an upward and downloads arrows on your watch respectively. (See Chapter 16: Your Activity from Apple Watch Series 5)

Cycle Tracking

The Apple Watch is made up of the new Cycle features to help women track their menstrual cycles . A discrete method of tracking the menstrual cycle is provided by the Cycle tracking app with tools to log various metrics.

It also provides notifications about period and fertility. (See Chapter 25: Chapter Cycle Tracking)

Noise

The Apple Watch can now monitor the noise level around you using the new watchOS 6 to protect you from noise and sound that can result in the damage of hearing over time.

The new Noise app helps in monitoring the noise and also measures the decibels of the ambient **environment with the use of the microphone of the Apple** watch.

It alerts you if the sound is over 90 decibels. This feature is also available on the Airpods and headphones making sure you are not listening to your music loudly.

See Chapter 27: Hearing Health—Measure Noise Levels with Apple Watch)

Mac Unlocking

In a situation where you are using your Apple watch with your Mac, there is now an available option to approve security prompts by tapping on the side button of your Apple watch as soon as you are prompted by MAC.

The Apple ID verification can now be displayed by the Apple watch to help with logging in, into your Apple account on a new browser or device

Taptic Chimes

This is a new Apple Watch feature which is designed to provide a silent Taptic touch on your wrist every hour.

Once the sounds are turned on, you will have access to hearing an audible chime. A taptic feature is also available in the settings that will help the Apple watch to tap a haptic version of the time.

These settings can be customized such that you will have a tab with various tab lengths in distinguishing minutes and hours. If the feature is enabled in your settings, all you need to do is to hold two fingers on your watch face and it will tell you the time. (See Chapter 9: Tell time on Apple Watch)

So, these are part of the new tips you are going to learn how to use in this detailed guide.

We do hope that the tips included in this book help you familiarize yourself with the new Apple Watch Series 5, so you can start using it like an expert.

Chapter 1: Setting Up your Apple Watch Series 5

Before we dive into this guide proper, I'd recommend you get conversant with the display buttons on your Apple watch. This will help you understand this guide proper. The image below will show you what each button in your Apple Watch represents:

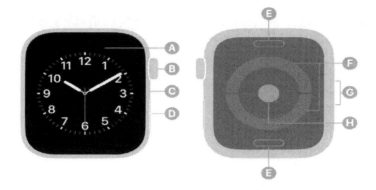

A: Represents the **Display button**.

A firm press on the **display button** will change the watch face. A firm Press will also let you see other features in any app.

B: Represents the **Digital Crown**.

- A Press on the **Digital Crown** will show you the Home screen or Watch face.
- You can also use it to zoom, scroll or make adjustments.
- If you Press and hold it for long, it will bring up Siri.

- It also functions as a Built-in electrode.

C: Represents the **Microphone**.

D: The Side button.

- A Press on the **side button** will bring up Dock.
- A Double-click will bring up Apple Pay.
- A Firm Press and hold will turn the Apple Watch on or off.
- You can also use it to make an emergency call.

  - So, in this guide, we will cover all that you need to know to help you become an expert in using your smart device. Without wasting much time, let's dive right into it.

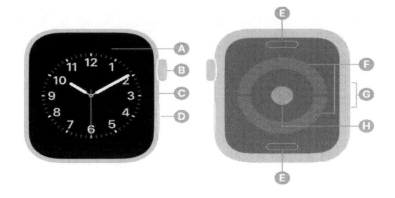

E: Stands   for   the   Band   release   button

F: The   Electrical   heart   sensor

G: Stands   for   the   Speaker/air   vents

F: The Optical heart sensor.

To download the latest iOS 13 version on your iPhone:

- Head to Settings
- Then to General
- After that, Software Update.
- From   there,   follow   the   on-screen instructions.

Once you're now sure that your iPhone is running the latest iOS, then you can now pair your Watch.

Pair Apple Watch with Your iPhone

Now that you have updated your Apple Watch to the latest version, the step you want to take is to pair it up with your iPhone.

Pairing up the Apple watch with your iPhone is like a match made in heaven.

- Wear your Apple Watch on your wrist.
- Adjust the band to enable the Apple Watch to fit snugly and comfortably on your wrist.
- Bring your iPhone close to your Apple Watch. Then wait for the Watch pairing screen to display on your iPhone.

- After that, tap Continue. Or you can also decide to open the Apple Watch app on your iPhone, thereafter, tap Pair New Watch.

- Ensure you position your iPhone so that your Apple Watch displays in the viewfinder in the Apple Watch app. This will allow for a flawless pairing of the two devices.

- After that, Tap Set Up Apple Watch and follow the instructions on the Apple Watch and iPhone to finish setup.

While the Watch is pairing with your iPhone, you will see some handy tips on how to interact with your Watch.

How to Unpair Apple Watch

To unpair apple watch:

- On your iPhone, open the Apple Watch app.

- Tap My Watch

- After that, tap your Apple Watch at the top of the screen.

- Tap the info button you will see close to the Apple Watch you want to unpair

- Then, tap Unpair Apple Watch.

How to Pair More Than One Apple Watch

Pairing another Apple Watch with the one you just paired is possible. All you need to do is to follow the same steps as the first one.

- Place your iPhone close to your Apple Watch

- Wait a bit for the Apple Watch pairing screen to appear on your iPhone.

- Then tap Pair.

Method 2

Open the Apple Watch app on your iPhone.

- Tap My Watch

- After that, tap your Apple Watch at the top of the screen.

- Then, Tap Pair New Watch.

- You will find the instructions you'll need to follow.

- Your iPhone will detect the paired Apple Watch you're wearing and connect to it automatically.

Pair Apple Watch to a New iPhone

If you pair your Apple Watch to your old iPhone and want to pair it with a new iPhone, follow these steps:

• First, use the iCloud Backup to have your currently paired iPhone backed up.

• Then set up your new iPhone.

- On the Apps & Data screen, select to restore from an iCloud backup, then choose the latest backup.

- When prompted, Move on with the iPhone setup, and select to use your Apple Watch with your new iPhone.

- When you complete the iPhone setup, your Apple Watch will prompt you to pair it to the new iPhone.

- Tap OK on your Apple Watch.

- After that, enter its passcode.

Chapter 2: How to Install the ECG Feature

Once you have updated your Apple operating system to WatchOS 5.1.2 and your iPhone to iOS 12.1.1, and you have paired them, then the next step is to install the ECG App.

According to Apple, you must be at least 22 years of age to take ECG on the Apple watch.

With that said, here are the steps to follow to help you install the ECG app successfully.

Step 1: Open the Health app on your iPhone after installing WatchOS 5.1.2. Once all this is in place, you should be prompted to set up the new ECG feature automatically.

Step 2: Fill in your date of birth to proceed, and then you will get an explanation from Apple on how the ECG app works.

Step 3: Once you're done with the setup, then you're ready to take your first ECG reading.

Make sure the watch is fitted snugly to your wrist, then Open the ECG app on your Apple Watch and ensure you rest your arm on a table or other stable object.

Hold your finger against the Digital Crown and wait for 30 seconds while you take the reading.

Step 4: Once completed, the test will display one of three potential results— atrial fibrillation, sinus rhythm, or inconclusive. The app will use an ECG or EKG reading to detect the upper and lower chambers of your heart, verifying whether or not they are in the right rhythm. If they are not, that means the wearer has atrial fibrillation, and they should immediately see a doctor.

Note: The ECG app will also transfer the result to your health app on your iPhone.

Within your iPhone, you can export the ECG test results in a PDF format in case you need to give them to your doctor, or you want to use them for another purpose.

While the ECG app can detect heart rate, it cannot identify a heart attack.

So, if you're having chest pain, blood clot, stroke or any other heart conditions, it won't detect it.

Also, note that you can only run the ECG app if you are in the United States.

While those are true, make sure you set the health notifications to get full advantage of the ECG feature. What this will do is to set up the Apple watch to occasionally look at your heart rate with a couple of other factors to see if there might be signs of Afib occurring.

How to SetUp Notifications

Here's how to set up the notifications.

• To do this, open up the apple watch app on your iPhone.

• Then scroll down to heart. You will see it right there where it says setup irregular rhythm notifications in health.

- If you click that, it will bring you to the health app, where you will get additional information about how the heart health alert iPhone Works.

How to Get the Best ECG Result

Although, taking an ECG (electrocardiogram) with the Apple Watch is straightforward and quick, there are some things that can create inaccuracies.

Here are a few useful tips to make sure you get the best results

- First, ensure your wrist and Apple watch are clean and dry.

- Move away from any electrical appliance that is plugged in to avoid electrical interference.

- Make sure the watch is snug and resting comfortably on your arms on a tabletop or on your lap when taking a reading.

• Ensure you're relaxed and you don't move too much.

• Your Apple Watch should be on the wrist as you select the Apple Watch app.

With all these tips in mind, you will be able to get the best ECG results.

How to share ECG Results with your Doctor

If you want to share your ECG result with your doctor, you can do that by:

• Locating the test app on your iPhone after taking your ECG test.

• Tap on the **Health icon** close to the bottom.

• After that, tap on Electrocardiogram (ECG).

- The next step is to tap on the ECG result you want to send to your doctor.

- Tap on "Export a PDF for Your Doctor."

- Then tap the button on the top right.

- Now select how you'd like to send the PDF (Mail, Messages, etc.).

So, next time you want to share your ECG report to your doctor, just Rinse and repeat the process.

Chapter 3: Charge Apple Watch

• Place the Apple Watch Magnetic Charging Cable Dock on a flat surface.

• Make sure the area is well-ventilated and

• Plug it into the power adapter.

• Then, Plug the adapter into a power outlet.

• To begin charging your Apple Watch, put the Magnetic Charging Cable on the back of your Apple Watch.

The concave end of the charging cable will snap to the back of your Apple Watch magnetically and aligns it properly.

• You'll hear a chime sound when it begins to charge (except your Apple Watch is in silent mode).

• Also, a green charging symbol will appear on the watch face, showing that the watch is charging and turns red when it needs power.

Note that you can charge your Apple Watch on its side or with its band open in a flat position.

If you're charging your Apple Watch with the Magnetic Charging Dock, just lay your Apple Watch on the dock.

Apple Watch Series 4

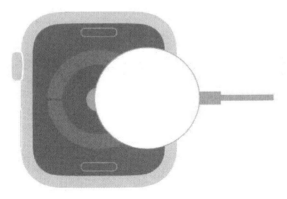

Check Remaining Power

To check the remaining power on your Apple watch:

- Touch and hold the bottom of the screen
- Then swipe up to open Control Center.

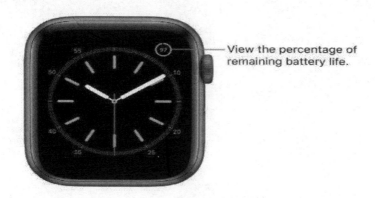

View the percentage of remaining battery life.

How to Save Power When the Battery Is Low

Your Apple watch gives you the option to save power by using the Power Reserve mode to extend the remaining battery.

The downside to this is that you won't be able to use your other apps even though the Watch displays the time.

To save Power:

- Touch and hold the bottom of the screen,

- Scroll up to open Control Center

- Then Tap the battery percentage, and drag the Power Reserve slider to the right.

Note that if your battery charge lowers to 10 percent, your Apple Watch alerts you and lets you enter the Power Reserve mode.

Also, your Apple Watch will enter the Power reserve Mode automatically when the power is extremely low.

Return to Normal Power Mode

To return to normal power mode, you need to Restart your Apple Watch.

• After that, Press and hold the side button to bring up the Apple logo.

- Make sure the battery is at least 10 percent charge before you can restart your Apple Watch.

You can also do this on your iPhone by Tapping on My Watch >General > Wake Screen.

Chapter 4: Always On Display

The Always On feature allows the watch screen to show the face and time of the Smartwatch, even when your wrist is down. The display works completely when you lift your hand.

1. Have the Settings app opened in your Apple smartwatch.

2. Press Display & Brightness, and click on Always On.

3. Switch on Always On.

4. After that, turn on Sensitive Complications to help you hide emails, calendar, heart rate, and more when your wrist is down.

Wake the Apple Watch display

The following are ways you can wake the screen of your Apple Watch:

- Raise your wrist. The Watch returns to sleep when your wrist is down.
- Click on the screen or press the Digital Crown.
- Turn up the Digital crown. To do so, open your Apple Watch, and click My Watch. From General, go to Wake Screen, and switch on Wake Screen on crown up.

If your Smartwatch's screen doesn't wake when your wrist is lifted, ensure you've chosen the correct wrist and watch mode. Also, your Apple Watch might need some charging if it does not unlock after you've clicked on the screen or moved the Digital Crown.

If you want the Wake screen on your Watch to be turned off even when you raise your wrist, then what you want to do is to:

1. Open the settings app

2. Then go to General > Wake Screen

3. From there turn off wake screen on wrist raise.

But if you want to temporarily stop your Apple Watch from waking even when your wrist is raised, simply use the theatre mode.

Wake to Your Last Activity

To set up your device to wake from the last app you used before it slept, do the following:

1. Go to Settings.

2. From General, go to Wake Screen, then enable the Wake Screen on Wrist Raise.

3. Swipe down and select to bring your Apple Watch to the last tool you've been using:

Always, under 60 minutes of the Last Usage, two Minutes of the Last Usage, or Never Unless in Session- this is for apps such as Workout, Maps or remotes.

If you want your Apple Watch to always wake up the watch face at all times (besides when a function is being used, select Never Unless in Session).

This could also be done with your Apple Watch app on your iPhone: Click on My Watch. Navigate to General > Wake Screen.

Keep the Apple Watch Display on longer

When you tap to wake your Apple Watch, it will **keep the Apple Watch Display on** for an extended period.

On the Apple Watch, Open Settings>General>Wake Screen, and click on Wake for 70 Seconds.

Chapter 5: Unlock Apple Watch with iPhone

You can unlock Apple Watch whenever you unlock your iPhone.

1. Open the Apple Watch app on your iPhone.

2. Tap Passcode, then turn on Unlock with iPhone. Your iPhone must be within normal Bluetooth range (about 33 feet or 10 meters) of your Apple Watch to unlock it.

Tip: Your Apple Watch passcode can be different from your iPhone passcode—infact, it's better to use different passcodes.

How to Change or Turn off Apple Watch Passcode

There's an easy way for you to modify or disable your passcode temporarily. But note that all your credit or debit cards loaded into Apple Pay will be erased if you choose to turn off passcode.

Here are the steps to do so:

• On your Apple Watch or iPhone, Open Settings in the Apple Watch App.

• Scroll down and tap Passcode

• Then, Tap Turn off or Change Passcode

• And that is it.

Unlock your Mac with Apple Watch

If you own a Mac with macOS High Sierra your Apple Watch can help you unlock your Mac instantly when it wakes from sleep.

First, you need to sign in to iCloud using your Apple ID on both your Apple Watch and Mac.

Pro Tip:

If you want to find out how old your Mac is, then click the Apple menu located in the top-left corner of your computer screen,

Then choose About This Mac.

You will see the year your Mac was made listed next to the model.

For instance, "MacBook Pro Retina, 13-inch, mid 2014)."

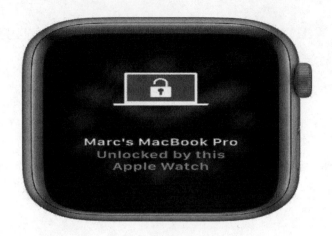

Turn on Auto Unlock

1. Choose the menu button on your mac

2. Go to system preferences.

3. Click on Security & Privacy

4. Then, click General.

5. Choose the "Allow Apple Watch to unlock your Mac" checkbox.

6. Ensure you follow the onscreen instructions if the two-factor

authentication is not turned on for your Apple ID

7. Then select the checkbox again.

8. Always remember to turn on Bluetooth and Wi-Fi on your Mac, while doing this.

Unlock your Mac

So, when your Watch is in your wrist, you can unlock **Wake up your Mac**, instead of typing in your password.

Lock Automatically

Turn on wrist detection to lock your watch automatically when you're not wearing it.

1. Open the Settings app on your Apple Watch.

2. Tap Passcode, then turn on Wrist Detection.

If you turn off Wrist Detection, each time you use Apple Pay on your Apple Watch, you'll be prompted to enter your passcode when you double-click the side button to authorize the payment. Also, Apple Watch Series 4 and later won't automatically make an emergency call even after it has detected a hard impact fall.

Lock Manually

1. Touch and hold the bottom of the screen, then swipe up to open Control Center.

2. Tap the Lock button.

Note: To manually lock your Apple Watch, you must turn off wrist detection. (Open the Settings app on your Apple Watch, tap Passcode, then turn off Wrist Detection.)

3. You must enter your passcode the next time you try to use your Apple Watch.

4. You can also lock your screen to avoid accidental taps during a workout. While using the Workout app on your Apple Watch, just swipe right, then tap Lock.

5. When you start a swimming workout with Apple Watch, your Apple Watch automatically locks the screen with Water Lock.

If You Forget Your Password

If you forget your password, you must erase your Apple Watch. You can do so in these ways:

1. Unpair your Apple Watch from your iPhone to erase your Apple Watch settings and passcode, then pair again.

2. Reset your Apple Watch and pair it again with your iPhone.

Erase Apple Watch after 10 Unlock attempts

To protect your information if your watch is lost or stolen, you can set Apple Watch to erase its data after 10 consecutive attempts to unlock it using the wrong password.

1. Open the Settings app on your Apple Watch.

2. Tap Passcode, then turn on Erase Data.

3. Change language and orientation on Apple Watch

4. Choose language or region

5. Open the Apple Watch app on your iPhone.

6. Tap My Watch, go to General > Language & Region, tap Custom, then tap Watch Language.

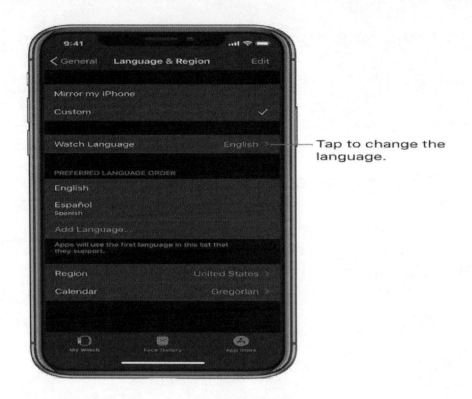

Tap to change the language.

7. Switch wrists or Digital Crown orientation

If you want to move your Apple Watch to your other wrist or prefer the Digital Crown on the other side, adjust your orientation settings so that raising your wrist wakes your Apple

Watch, and turn the Digital Crown to move things in the direction you expect.

8. Open the Settings app on your Apple Watch.

9. Go to General > Orientation.

You can also open the Apple Watch app on your iPhone, tap My Watch, then go to General > Watch Orientation.

Chapter 6: How to Remove, Change Apple Watch Bands

Before you change your Apple Watch band ensure the new band has the same size as the old one.

The new band must correspond and be compatible with your Apple Watch case size.

Also know that Bands for 40mm and 38mm cases work fine with each other. And bands for 44mm and 42mm cases will work well with each other. And any band designed for a season, will work for previous models as well.

- To change and remove bands, Press the band release button on your Apple Watch.
- Then remove the band by sliding it across.
- After removing it, slide the new band in.

Please do not force a band into the slot. All you need to do is to press the band release button again if you are having difficulty removing or inserting the band.

Keep this in mind that your Apple watch needs to be fastened snugly to fit your wrist to offer the best performance.

Also, the bottom/back of the Apple watch should have contact with your skin for features like fall detection, the heart rate sensor, and haptic notifications.

So your watch must be comfortable while wearing and lets the sensors do their job.

Ensure your Apple Watch is well tightened during workouts. But loosen the band when you're through with the workout.

Chapter 7: Apps on Apple Watch

Your Apple Watch comes with apps that let you have access to different communications, like, health, fitness and timekeeping tasks.

It also allows you to install third-party apps you have on your iPhone, and let you add new apps from the App Store. All your apps are on a single Home screen.

Use the Dock on your Apple Watch

The dock feature allows you to quickly open your favorite apps or go from one app to another with less hassle. To use the Dock feature:

• Open an app from the Dock

• And Press the side button.

• Then Swipe up or down, or turn the Digital Crown.

• After that, Tap to open an app.

• Scroll all the way down, and tap All Apps to take you to the Home screen.

• Press the side button to close the Dock.

Choose Which Apps Appear In the Dock

The Dock can let you know your 10 most favorite apps or most recent apps.

If you choose **Recents**, your apps will display in the order that you opened them. If you choose Favorites, you can select the apps that display, but your most recently used app still shows up at the top of the Dock.

If it's not yet already a favorite, then tap Keep in Dock to add it.

So how do you choose what appears?

- On your iPhone, open the Apple Watch app.

- Tap the My Watch tab,

- And then tap Dock: tap favorites or recent.

Choose Your Favorite Apps

To arrange the Dock by Favorites, choose which apps to appear or remove by;

- Opening the Apple Watch app on your iPhone.

- Tap the My Watch tab

• Then tap Dock.

• Ensure that the Favorites App is selected.

• Then Tap Edit.

To delete apps, tap the - (Minus) icon, and press Remove.

To add apps,

• Tap the + (plus) icon, which will let you add up to 10 apps.

• If you want to rearrange apps, touch and hold the 3 dashes next to an app.

• Then drag up or down.

• To save your changes, tap Done.

To Remove an app from the Dock:

• Open the Dock.

• Then go to an app

• And swipe left.

• Then Tap the x icon to remove all apps.

Rearrange Your Apps in Grid View

To arrange your apple watch in gridview:

• Press the Digital Crown On your Apple Watch to go to the Home screen.

• If you notice that the screen is in list view, press the display firmly and tap Grid View.

- Ensure you Touch and hold an app until they all jiggle,

- After that, drag it to a new location.

- When you're done, Press the Digital Crown.

You can also do this on your iPhone by:

- Opening your Apple Watch app on your iPhone

- Once you do that, tap My Watch.

- Then tap App Layout.

- Touch and hold an app icon.

- After that, drag it to a new location.

Do not forget that the Apps on apple watch are arranged in alphabetical order.

Remove a Third-Party App from Apple Watch

You can remove a third-party app in both Grid view and List view.

Grid View

● Touch and hold the app icon on the Home screen to bring up an X on the icon.

● Once you see the X icon, tap the X to delete the app from your Apple Watch.

● But it will still be on your paired iPhone, unless you remove it from there too.

List View

● In list view, Swipe the app to the left,

● Then tap the Trash button to delete it from your Apple Watch.

- It will still remain on your paired iPhone, unless you remove it from there, too.

Yes, You can still remove an app from your Apple Watch and iPhone at the same time.

- Touch and hold the app icon On your iPhone, to bring up an X on the icon,

- Then tap the X to erase the app from your Apple Watch and iPhone.

- If you want to restore an app, you've removed, just download it to your iPhone from the App Store.

Adjust App Settings

This is pretty straightforward:

- On your iPhone, open the Apple Watch app.

- Tap My Watch.

78

- Then scroll down to view apps you've installed.

- The next step is to Tap an app to change its settings.

To set any restrictions on your iPhone go to Settings > Screen Time > Content & Privacy Restrictions. This will definitely affect your Apple Watch also.

For instance, if you have your iPhone watch Camera disabled, the Camera Remote icon will be removed from the Apple Watch Home screen.

Check Storage Used by Apps

To do this:

- On your iPhone, open the Apple Watch app.

- Tap My Watch,

- And go to General, then Usage.

With that, you will be able to know the amount of storage used by the app.

How to Get more apps on the App Store on Apple Watch

With the Series 5, you can get more apps from the App Store. The new watchOS 6 now gives you the flexibility to get Apps downloaded directly on the App store on your watch without having to use your iPhone.

This new featured App Store enables you to search for Apps or make use of the Siri voice assistance to get your searches done.

So, to get Apps from App Store:

1. On your Apple Watch, navigate to the App Store

2. Change the Digital Crown to search for recommended apps.

4. Press **'See All'** below to get a list of apps or simply select a category.

5. Click 'Get' to download a free app or click on the amount to buy an app.

If you have already paid for the app, the download button will be displayed. You must have the iOS version of some apps on your iPhone before you can download them.

To locate a particular app, click on the Search area located at the screen top. Enter the space with the name of the app using Dictation Scribble.

When you click on a category, you will find popular categories of apps there.

Keep in mind that Scribble is only available in limited languages. Also, you will be charged for cellular data when you use the Apple Watch with cellular.

Install Apps You Already Have On IPhone

If your iPhone device has a WatchOS app, the apps on your device will be seen on your Apple Watch home screen. This is because, it has been automatically installed. To select the apps you want to install:

1. Open the WatchOS app on your iPhone
2. Press 'My Watch' and press 'General'. Here, you will switch off the Automatic App Install.
3. Click on **'My Watch '** and drag the screen down to **'Available Apps'**
4. Press the install button next to the app.

Download the apps on your iPhone's App Store

- From your iPhone, navigate to the App Store app.

- Search for "Apple Watch" from the search bar

Download the app by clicking on the 'Get' button.

Tip: To navigate to a particular app faster, write the name on the search field provided you know the name.

Chapter 8: Make Phone Calls on Apple Watch

You can very well receive phone calls on your Apple Watch. When you feel or hear the notification, you want to raise your wrist to see who's calling. Then Tap the Answer button to talk by using the built-in microphone and speaker.

Aside from that, you can also send a call to voicemail someone; just tap the red Decline button you see in the incoming call notification.

Apart from answering calls on your Apple Watch, you can also make calls too.

Ask Siri. Say something like:

"Call Max" "Dial 566 555 2049"

"Call Pete FaceTime audio"

- To Make a call, Open the Phone app on your Apple Watch.

- Tap on Contacts,

- Then turn the Digital Crown to scroll.

- Tap the contact you'd like to call,

- After that, tap the phone button.

Tips to Keep in Mind:

- To call the person you recently spoken with, tap Recents, then tap a contact.

- To call someone you've selected as a favorite in the Phone app on your iPhone, tap Favorites, then tap a contact

- To enter a phone number on Apple Watch, Open the Phone app on your Apple Watch.

Then Tap Keypad, and enter the number. After that, tap the Call button.

• The keypad also gives you access to enter a phone extension during a call. All you need to do is to scroll up and tap the Keypad button.

• To adjust call volume, you need to Tap the volume symbols on the screen or turn the Digital Crown.

• Tap the Mute button to mute the call in case you're listening on a conference call.

• Enter a phone extension, Swipe up, then tap Keypad, and enter the extension.

• To Switch a call an audio device, simply Swipe up, and tap the Audio Output button. After that, choose a device.

• In a FaceTime Audio call, you can easily adjust the volume, mute the call when you tap the Mute button or scroll up voicemail an audio destination.

• You can Listen to voicemail and get a notification if a caller leaves a voicemail. Once you get the alert, tap the Play button in the notification to listen.

If you want to hear voicemail at a later date, open the Phone app on your Apple Watch, and tap Voicemail.

• To delete the voicemail

Make calls over Wi-Fi

If your cellular carrier comes with Wi-Fi calling, you can utilize your Apple Watch to make and receive calls via Wi-Fi instead of using the cellular network—even if your paired iPhone is turned off or not with you.

To have a fluid performance, ensure that your Apple Watch is within the range of a Wi-Fi network that you have connected your iPhone in the past.

So to enable Wi-Fi calling on your iPhone:

• On your iPhone, go to Settings, then to Phone.

• Tap Wi-Fi Calling, then turn on both Wi-Fi Calling

• After that, Add Wi-Fi Calling For Other Devices.

Enable Wi-Fi Calling On Your Apple Watch:

• Open the Apple Watch app on your iPhone,

• Tap My Watch,

• Then tap Phone,

• Next, turn on Wi-Fi Calls. Ensure you enable Wi-Fi calling on your iPhone if you don't see the setting.

Make an Emergency Phone Call on Apple Watch

Another nice thing about the Apple Watch is that it lets you make an emergency call in case you quickly need help.

To make an emergency call follow these steps:

• You have to Press and hold the side button until you see the sliders appear.

• After that, drag the Emergency SOS slider to the right.

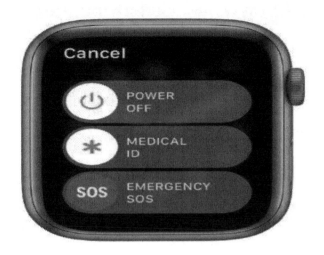

• After following those steps above, Your Apple Watch then calls the emergency services in your area—For instance, 911.

• However, some countries require their citizens to press a keypad number to conclude the call.) After completing the call, the Apple Watch now alerts the emergency contacts that they made a call and sends them their current location (if available).

- So make sure you Press and keep holding the side button until you see that your Apple Watch beeps and starts a countdown.

- When it has completed the countdown, your Apple Watch calls emergency services.

- Keep this in mind that the Apple Watch beeps even when in silent mode. So, in the case of an emergency and you don't want the beeping sound to make noise, utilize the Emergency SOS slider to call emergency services without any countdown.

If you want to stop your Apple Watch to automatically begin the emergency countdown anytime you press and hold the side button,

- Turn off Automatic Dialing by Opening the Apple Watch app on your iPhone.

- Tap My Watch

- Then tap Emergency SOS

- After that, turn off Hold Side Button. Know that you can still make an emergency call using the Emergency SOS slider.

Cancel an Emergency Call

If you accidentally start an emergency call:

- Firmly press the display.

- Then tap End Call to cancel.

Add an Emergency Contact

You can add an emergency contact with these steps:

- On your IPhone, Open the Health app.

- Tap Medical ID,

- And then tap Edit.

- Then Tap "add emergency contact,"

- Finally, tap Done to have your changes saved.

Chapter 9: Tell time on Apple Watch

There are several ways to tell time with your Apple Watch.

Raise your wrist: The time appears on the watch face, in the clock in grid view, and in the top-right corner of most apps.

Hear the time: Open the Settings app on your Apple Watch, tap Clock, then turn on Speak Time. Hold two fingers on the watch face to hear the time.

Apple Watch can also play chimes on the hour. In the Settings app on Apple Watch, tap Clock, then turn on Chimes. Tap Sounds to choose Bells or Birds.

Feel the time: To feel the time tapped out on your wrist, open the Settings app on your Apple Watch, tap Clock, tap Taptic Time, turn on Taptic Time, then choose an option.

Use Taptic Time

Apple Watch can tap out the time on your wrist with a series of distinct taps.

1. Open the Settings app on your Apple Watch.

2. Tap Clock, scroll up, then tap Taptic Time.

3. Turn on Taptic Time, then choose a setting—Digits, Terse, or Morse Code.

Digits: Apple Watch long taps for every 10 hours, short taps for each following hour, long taps for every 10 minutes, then short taps for each following minute.

Terse: Apple Watch long taps for every five hours, short taps for the remaining hours, then long taps for each quarter hour.

Morse Code: Apple Watch taps each digit of the time in Morse code.

You can also configure Taptic Time on iPhone.

Open the Apple Watch app on iPhone, tap My Watch, go to Clock > Taptic Time, then turn it on.

Discreetly View the Time

Tapping on the screen, will let you see the time without raising your hand.

The problem with this method is that it can be too bright sometimes.

The best way out is to gently turn the Digital Crown, so it carefully and slowly illuminate the screen. When you've seen the time, turn the Digital crown backward to make the screen dark.

Chapter 10: Use Smarter Siri on Apple Watch

You can use Siri to carry out tasks and deliver answers on your Apple Watch 5. Thanks to the introduction of watchOS 6, you can now ask Siri to select a song and get an immediate Shazam result.

It is also possible to make a general inquiry from Siri; your Apple Watch will produce a list of search results with brief descriptions. Click 'Open Page' to check out any of the page on your Apple Watch. You can also inquire some things to do from Siri.

Ask Siri. Give out a command like:

• "Begin a 1-hour outdoor walk"

- "Tell Kathleen I'm not coming"

- "Open the Heart Rate app"

- "What rhythm is this?"

- "What causes suicides?"

- "What kinds of things can I ask you?"

Interact with Siri

Get your requests over to Siri using any of the following gestures:

- Lift your wrist and talk to your Series 5 Watch.

Switch off the 'Raise To Speak' feature by opening the settings on your Apple Watch; Press 'Siri' and then switch off 'Raise To Speak'

- Before asking, say 'Hey Siri'

You can turn this particular speech off by opening settings on your watch; click 'Siri and then switch off the 'Listen for "Hey Siri"' feature.

1. Click the Siri button on the watch face of Siri

2. Keep holding the Digital Crown and the listening indicator will appear at the screen's bottom. Ask Siri your request before leaving the Digital Crown.

You can switch off this feature by opening settings on your watch; Press Siri and then switch off 'Press Digital Crown'

Tip: bring down your wrist after your request. Siri will give a tap sound as an indicator of his response.

If Siri asks a question that you have to respond, keep your hold on the Digital Crown to speak. This can also be used to continue a conversation with Siri.

Siri's response is similar to iOS and macOS. If you connect a bluetooth headphone to your Apple Watch, you will be able to hear the Siri's response.

Keep in Mind that the Apple Watch must be connected to Wi-Fi or Cellular before you can use Siri. You will be charged for the Data used.

Chapter 11: Manage Your Notifications

You can now easily manage your notifications on your Apple Watch.

This means you can now decide to revoke an app's notification privileges from the lock screen, and gain extra controls over those apps that keep on sending you alert messages almost all the time.

One of the massive improvements to notifications on watchOS 6 is that you can now group together alerts from the same app. Instead of listing each alert separately, one card is displayed per app, and if there are more alerts, you can see the silhouette of more alerts underneath — much like a stack of paper.

Tap on the top alert to ungroup the alerts and view them individually. When you view your list of alerts, swipe to the left on an individual alert.

You can clear that particular alert with a tap on the "X," or view new options by selecting the three-dot button. Choose whether you'd like the apps' alerts to be delivered quietly, or not at all.

To **Deliver Quietly** simply means that the alerts will still display in the notification center on your watch, but you won't receive an alert that there's a new notification.

Selecting Turn Off on Apple Watch stops the app from sending alerts to your wrist.

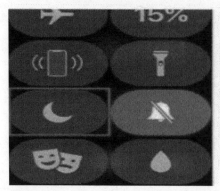 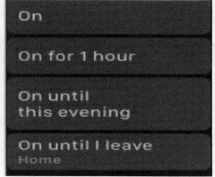

While Apple might have introduced the **Do Not Disturb** mode in iOS 13, it has also extended this feature to the Apple Watch. Specifically, whenever you manually enable DND from Control Center (swipe up from the bottom of the screen when viewing your watchface), you're given the option to set DND to stay on until you turn it off, expire in an hour, later that evening, when you leave your current location.

Respond To a Notification When It Arrives

If you hear or feel a notification, raise your wrist to view it.

1. Turn the Digital Crown to scroll to the bottom of the notification, then tap a button there.

2. You can also tap the app icon in the notification to open the corresponding app.

3. To clear a notification, swipe down on it. Or scroll to the bottom of the notification, then tap Dismiss.

The icon for the app associated with the notification appears at the top left. You can tap it to open the app.

See Notifications You Haven't Responded To

If you don't respond to a notification when it arrives, it's saved in Notification Center. A red dot at the top of your watch face shows you have an unread notification. To view it, follow these steps:

1. From the watch face, swipe down to open Notification Center. From other screens, touch and hold the top of the screen, then swipe down.

Note: You can't open Notification Center when viewing the Home screen on your Apple Watch.

Instead, press the Digital Crown to go to the watch face or open an app, then open Notification Center.

2. Swipe up or down or turn the Digital Crown to scroll the notifications list.

3. Tap the notification to read or respond to it.

To clear a notification from Notification Center without reading it, swipe it to the left, then tap X. To clear all notifications, firmly press the display, then tap Clear All.

4. If you group notifications, tap a group to open it, then tap a notification.

Swipe down to view unread notifications.

Choose How Notifications Are Delivered

By default, the notification settings for the apps on your Apple Watch mirror the settings on your iPhone. But you can customize how some apps display notifications.

1. Open the Apple Watch app on your iPhone.

2. Tap My Watch, then tap Notifications.

3. Tap the app (for example, Messages), tap Custom, then choose an option. Options may include:

4.   Allow   Notifications: The   app displays notifications   in   Notification Center.

5.   Send   to   Notification Center: Notifications   are   sent   directly   to Notification Center   without   your Apple Watch   making   a   sound or displaying the notification.

Apps   that   support direct   delivery   to Notification   Center   include   Activity, Breathe,   Calendar,   Mail,   Messages, Podcasts, Reminders, and Wallet.

Notifications Off: The app sends no notifications.

You can also manage notifications preferences directly on your Apple Watch by swiping left on a notification and tapping the More button. Options may include:

Deliver Quietly: Notifications are sent directly to Notification Center without your Apple Watch making a sound or displaying the notification.

To see and hear these notification alerts again, swipe left on a notification, tap the More button, then tap Deliver Prominently.

Turn Off on Apple Watch: The app sends no notifications.

Notification settings on Apple Watch. The top button reads "Deliver Quietly," and the button below reads "Turn Off on Apple Watch."

Use Notification Grouping

For each app on your Apple Watch that supports notifications, you can choose how notifications are grouped.

1. Open the Apple Watch app on your iPhone.

2. Tap My Watch, then tap Notifications.

Tap an app, tap Custom, then tap Notification Grouping. Options include:

Off: Notifications aren't grouped.

Automatically: Your Apple Watch uses information from the app to create separate groups. For example, News notifications are grouped by the channels you follow—CNN, Washington Post, and People.

By App: The entire app's notifications are grouped.

Silence all notifications on Apple Watch

Touch and hold the bottom of the screen, swipe up to open Control Center, then tap the silent mode button.

You still feel a tap when a notification arrives. To prevent sound and taps, touch and hold the bottom of the screen, swipe up to open Control Center, then tap the Do Not Disturb button.

Tip: When you get a notification, you can quickly mute your Apple Watch by resting the palm of your hand on the watch display for at least three seconds. You'll feel a tap to confirm that mute is on. Make sure you turn on Cover to Mute in the Apple Watch app on your iPhone—tap My Watch, then go to Sounds & Haptics.

Keep Notifications On Apple Watch Private

When you raise your wrist to see a notification, you see a quick summary, then full details a few seconds later. For example, when a message arrives, you see who it's from first, then the message appears.

To stop the full notification from appearing unless you tap it, follow these steps:

1. Open the Apple Watch app on your iPhone.

2. Tap My Watch, then tap Notifications.

3. Turn on Notification Privacy.tr

Chapter 12: How to Connect To a Wi-Fi Network with Your Apple Watch

In an earlier version of Apple Watch, you could only use WiFi networks that are tied to your iPhone.

But with the recent update, you can now browse Wi-Fi networks and use them from Apple Watch. If you want to connect your Apple watch to a new network;

1. Open the Settings app on your wrist,

2. Then Tap Wi-Fi, and choose an available network from the list.

3. After that, type the password by using the screen's gesture.

4. And that is it. Enjoy your free Wi-Fi on the go.

Forget a Network

1. Open the Settings app on your Apple Watch.

2. Tap Wi-Fi, then tap the name of the network you're connected to.

3. Tap Forget This Network.

4. If you rejoin that network at a later time, you must reenter its password if it requires one.

Chapter 13: Hand off tasks from Apple Watch

Handoff lets you move from one device to another without losing focus on what you're doing. For example, even though you can reply to email using the Mail app on your Apple Watch, you might want to switch to your iPhone so you can reply using the onscreen keyboard. Follow these steps to use Handoff.

1. Unlock your iPhone.

2. Double-click the Home button to show the App Switcher. (On iPhone X and later, swipe up from the bottom edge and pause to show the App Switcher.)

3. Tap the button that appears at the bottom of the screen to open the same item on your iPhone.

Tip: If you don't see a button in App Switcher, make sure Handoff is turned on for your iPhone in Settings > General > Handoff.

Handoff is on by default. To disable it, open the Apple Watch app on your iPhone, tap My Watch, tap General, then turn off Enable Handoff.

Handoff works with Activity, Alarm, Calendar, Home, Mail, Maps, Messages, Music, News, Phone, Podcasts, Reminders, Settings, Siri, Stocks, Stopwatch, Timer, Wallet, Weather, and World Clock.

For Handoff to work, your Apple Watch must be connected to your paired iPhone.

If you have a Mac with OS X 10.10 or later installed, you can also hand off from your Apple Watch to your Mac.

Chapter 14: Use Apple Watch with A Cellular Network

Apple Watches with cellular connection sharing the same carrier used by your iPhone can make calls, reply to messages, use Walkie-Talkie, stream music and do podcasts, receive notifications, and more, even when you don't have your iPhone or a Wi-Fi connection.

Note: Cellular service is not available in all areas or with all carriers.

Add Apple Watch to Your Cellular Plan

You can activate cellular service on your Apple Watch by following the instructions during the initial setup. To activate service later, follow these steps:

1. Open the Apple Watch app on your iPhone.

2. Tap My Watch, then tap Cellular.

3. Follow the instructions to learn more about your carrier service plan and activate cellular for your Apple Watch with cellular. See the Apple Support article Set up cellular on your Apple Watch.

Turn Cellular Off Or On

Your Apple Watch with cellular uses the best network connection available to it—your iPhone when it's nearby, a Wi-Fi network that you've connected to previously on your iPhone, or a cellular connection. You can turn cellular off—to save battery power, for example. Just follow these steps:

1. Touch and hold the bottom of the screen, then swipe up to open Control Center.

2. Tap the Cellular button, then turn Cellular off or on.

3. The Cellular button turns green when your Apple Watch has a

cellular connection and your iPhone isn't nearby.

Note: Turning on cellular for extended periods uses more battery power.

Check Cellular signal Strength

Try one of the following when connected to a cellular network:

Use the Explorer watch face, which uses green dots to show cellular signal strength. Four dots is a good connection. One dot is poor.

1. Open Control Center. The green dots at the top left show the cellular connection status.

2. Add the Cellular complication to the watch face.

3. Check cellular data usage

4. Open the Apple Watch app on your iPhone.

5. Tap My Watch, then tap Cellular.

Chapter 15: Apple Watch Faces and their Features

The Apple Watch now features a lot of easy ways to customize watch faces. Apple watch also gives you the option to add complications (special feature) to your Watch face. For example:

Activity Analog

This watch face will appear in traditional analog clock to show your activity progress.

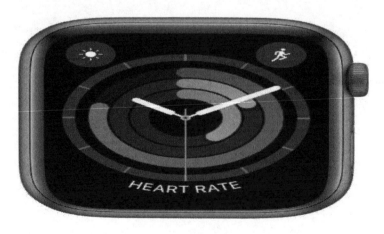

Breathe

This watch face lets you relax and breathe mindfully. To begin, tap the display.

Customizable features: Style (Calm, Activity, and Focus. Available complications include: Activity, Alarm, Battery, Breathe, Calendar, Date, Find My Friends, etc.

Siri

The Siri watch face enables Siri to display important information, like your next appointment, the score of a game played by your favorite team or a traffic situation.

Tap for Siri.

TUE 10

Turn the Digital Crown to see more information.

Tap to open.

Create A Photo Face On Your IPhone

1. Start by opening the Photos app on your iPhone.

2. Then tap a photo, and also tap on the button

3. Lastly, tap Create Watch Face. You can then choose to create a Photo watch face or a Kaleidoscope watch face.

Ensure that the photos are in your synced album or you might not see any pictures.

• You can swipe to any watch face you want, then tap it.

• With the watch face showing, press the display firmly,

• Then tap Customize.

• Swipe left all the way to the end. If a face features complications, they're shown on the last screen.

• Tap a complication to select it,

• Turn the Digital Crown to choose a new one like: Heart Rate, or Activity for example.

- When you're done, press the Digital Crown to have your changes saved,

- Then tap the face to switch to it.

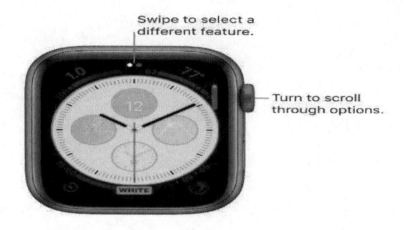

Swipe to select a different feature.

Turn to scroll through options.

Add Complications from other apps.

You can also add complications for many apps you take from the App Store, alongside the built-in complications that bring up information stocks, such as weather, or news.

To make these complications available whenever you want to customize a face:

- Open the Apple Watch app on your iPhone.

- Then Tap My Watch,

- Followed by Complications.

- Add a preferred watch face to your collection

- You can now create your own collection of custom faces

- With the current watch face showing, press the display firmly.

- Then you want to Swipe left all the way to the end,

- Then tap the New button (+).

- After that, Swipe up and down to browse watch faces,

- The next step is to tap the one you want to add.

- Once you add it, you can customize the watch face.

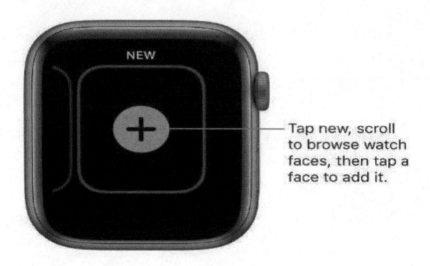

Tap new, scroll to browse watch faces, then tap a face to add it.

View Your Collection

Did you know that you can view your watch faces at a glance? To do so:

- Open the Apple Watch app on your iPhone.
- Tap My Watch,

- Swipe through your collection below My Faces.
- tap Edit, in case you want to rearrange the order of your collection.
- The next step is to drag the Reorder icon next to a watch face up or down.

Delete a Face from Your Collection

To remove a face from your collection is quite easy:

- With the current watch face showing, you want to firmly press the display.
- Swipe to the face you want to remove, then swipe it up
- And tap Remove.
- Or, open the Apple Watch app on your iPhone.
- Then tap My Watch,

- Then tap Edit in the My Faces area.
- Next, Tap the Delete button next to the watch faces you'd like to remove,
- Then tap Remove.

You can also do this while browsing the Photos app on your Apple Watch. Select any photo and tap on the Create Watch Face.

Chapter 16: Your Activity from Apple Watch Series 5

You can keep your fitness routine on track with your friends and family, a coach or a trainer. The Activity competition in the new WatchOS 6 allows you to challenge a friend to a seven-day competition.

Both of you will earn points per the percentage of Activity rings you close.

To add a friend:

1. On your iPhone, open the Activity app.

2. Tap Sharing, then tap Get Started,

3. Next, tap the Add button in the top-right corner.

4. Fill in your friend's name, and tap Send.

When your friend accepts your invitation, you will see their activity and they can also see yours.

But if you want to remove a friend,

1. Open the Activity app on your iPhone,

2. Tap Sharing, then tap a friend.

3. After that, tap Remove Friend

To check your friends' progress:

1. On your Apple Watch, open the Activity app.

2. Then, Swipe left, and turn the Digital Crown to scroll your friends list.

3. Then Tap friends to see their progress for the day.

In case you discover that your friend's aren't meeting up with their set goal, you can keep them motivated by sending a message. To do this:

1. Open the Activity app on your Apple Watch.

2. Then Swipe left, and turn the Digital Crown to scroll to the bottom.

3. Tap the "**Send message to all,**" From there, write your message.

4. Tap the friend in your friends list to write a message to a specific friend.

5. When you are done with the message, scroll to the bottom, and tap Send Message.

How to View Activity Summary on Apple Watch

To do this:

- Open the Activity app On Apple Watch

- Press the screen firmly

• Then Tap on Weekly Summary. This will show you your summary of the week's activity. The screen will display stats such as the amount of steps calories, and the distance you've accumulated throughout the week.

Check your trends

The trend tab demonstrates your regular trend information for active calorie intake, workout minutes, standing hours, standing minutes, walking distance, and more.

This you will find in the iPhone Activity App with iOS 13. The trend information depends on how these parameters have shifted relative to the last 365 days over the past 90 days.

To see how you're trending, follow these steps:

1. Go to the Activity app on your iPhone.

2. Click **'Trends'**. You will find this below the screen.

When the trend arrow faces up for a specific metric, it shows that your fitness level has been maintained or improved.

If an arrow turns down, it means your average of 90 days has begun to decrease for that metric. You will receive instruction that will motivate you to transform the trend around (i.e. "Walk an additional quarter of a mile a day).

See Your Awards

Using your Apple Watch can help you win awards for private documents, streaks, and significant achievements. Follow these initiatives to see all your prizes, including

Activity Competition awards and awards to which you are making strides:

1. Go to the Activity app on your Apple Watch.

2. To view the Awards screen, navigate to left two times

3. Check your awards by scrolling up. Click an award to find out about it.

You can also view awards on your iPhone. To do that, Open the Activity app, then tap Awards at the bottom of the screen.

Adjust Your Goals

1. On your Smartwatch open the activity application

2. Long press the screen, and click Change Move Goal.

You will be notified every Monday of your accomplishments of the past week, and you can change your objectives for the following week. Your Apple Watch will indicate objectives, depending on your past results.

Control Activity Reminders

Reminders also assist you to achieve your objectives. This will give you an idea of whether you are on the right path or behind your objectives.

Follow these measures to choose which reminders and notifications you would rather see:

1. Open Apple Watch app on your Apple iPhone device, and click on **My Watch**.

2. Click Activity, and set up your reminders.

Suspend Daily Coaching

If you want to switch your activity reminders off, execute the following steps:

1. Open your Apple smartwatch app with your iPhone, and click on **My Watch.**

2. Tap on Activity, and switch Daily Coaching off.

Wake to your Last Activity

To set up Smartwatch to wake from the last app you used before it turned off:

1. Go to Settings.

2. From General go to Wake Screen, then enable the Wake Screen on Wrist Raise.

3. Swipe down and select to bring your Apple Watch to the last tool you've been using: Just, under 60 minutes of the Last Usage, two Minutes of the Last Usage, or Never Unless in Session- this is for applications such as Workout, Maps or remotes.

If you want your Apple Watch to warm up to the smartwatch face at all times (besides when a function is being used) select Never Unless in Session).

This could also be done with your iPhone's Apple Watch application: Click on My Watch. Navigate to General > Wake Screen.

Chapter 17: Use Apple Watch to Breathe Mindfully

You can have a few minutes a day to relax and focus on your breathing using the Breathe app on your Apple Watch.

- To start a breathe session, Open the Breathe app on your Apple Watch.

- Then Tap Start, and inhale slowly as the animation grows, and exhale as it shrinks.

Set the Duration of a Breathe Session

• On your Apple Watch, Open the Breathe app.

• Then increase your duration by Turning the Digital Crown.

• You can choose a time between 1--5 minutes.

• You can set this as your default duration, by opening the Apple Watch app on your iPhone.

• Tap My Watch, and tap Breathe,

• Then turn on Use Previous Duration.

Adjust Breathe Settings

You can customize the way you want to frequently get breathe reminders, change your breathe rate and mute breathe reminders for the day. To do this:

• Open the Apple Watch app on your iPhone

145

- Then, Tap My Watch.

- Tap Breathe.

- After that, you can Set breathe reminders by Tapping Breathe Reminders.

- You can Mute breathe reminders by Turning on "Mute for today."

- You can adjust your breathing rate by tapping Breathe Rate to adjust the number of breaths per minute.

See Your Heart Rate During Breathe Sessions

You can do this by;

- Tapping on the Health Data.

- Then tap Heart.

- From there, Swipe left on heart rate to view Breathe.

Use the Breathe Watch Face

By adding the Breathe watch face, you can gain quick access to the breathe sessions.

● First, firmly press the display with the current watch face showing.

● Swipe left all the way to the end.

● Then tap the New button (+).

● After that, Turn the Digital Crown to choose Breathe.

● Then tap to add it.

● Now, you can then Tap the watch face to start a breathing session.

Chapter 18: Use Calculator on Apple Watch

The Calculator app allows you to do basic arithmetic stuff.

Ask Siri."What is 86 times 4?" or "What's 100 percent of 425?"

Perform a quick calculation

1. Just open the Calculator app on your Apple Watch.

2. Then you tap the numbers and operators to get a result.

Split the Check and Calculate a Tip

1. Simply open the Calculator app on your Apple Watch.

2. Key in the total amount of the bill, before tapping Tip.

3. You then turn the Digital Crown to choose a tip percentage.

4. Just tap People, before turning the Digital Crown to enter the number of people sharing the bill.

The results you get should show the tip amount, the total amount, and how much each person is to pay if the bill is split equally.

Note that the Tip feature is not available in every region.

Chapter 19: Check and Update Your Calendar on Apple Watch

You can schedule events on the apple watch using the Calendar app.

To view calendar events on Apple Watch:

● You can either Open the Calendar app on your Apple Watch, or tap a calendar event on the watch face or tap the date.

● Turn the Digital Crown to scroll through scheduled events.

• Tap any event to view details like location, time, invitee status, and notes.

• Tap the time in the top-right corner to go back to the next event.

Chapter 20: How to Use Apple Watch as Camera Remote

To go about this, open the Camera app on your Apple Watch.

This will bring up the Camera on your iPhone instantly. From there, tap on the shutter button on Apple Watch to use the timer or take a picture.

Use Camera and timer on Apple Watch

If you want to position your iPhone for a photo and then take the photo from a distance, you can use your Apple Watch to view the iPhone camera image and take the photo. You can also use your Apple Watch to set a shutter timer— this gives you time to lower your wrist and raise your eyes when you're in the shot.

To function as a camera remote, your Apple Watch needs to be within normal Bluetooth range of your iPhone (about 33 feet or 10 meters).

Ask Siri. Say something like: "Take a picture."

Start the timer.

Take a photo.

Take A Photo

Open the Camera app on your Apple Watch.

Position your iPhone to frame the shot using your Apple Watch as a viewfinder.

To adjust exposure, tap the key area of the shot in the preview on your Apple Watch. To take the shot, tap the Shutter button.

To take a Live Photo, firmly press the display, then tap Live .The photo is captured in Photos on your iPhone, but you can review it on your Apple Watch.

Choose A Different Camera Or Camera Mode

Choose a different camera: To switch between the rear-facing camera and the front-facing camera on your iPhone, open the Camera app on your Apple Watch, firmly press the display, then tap Flip .Choose a different camera mode: Open the Camera app on your iPhone, then swipe to choose Time-Lapse, Slo-Mo, Video, Portrait, or Square. Control flash, shutter timer, and HDR with Apple Watch.

Turn the flash on or off: Open the Camera app on your Apple Watch, firmly press the display, tap Flash , then tap Auto, On, or Off.

Use the shutter timer: Open the Camera app on your Apple Watch, then tap the Timer button on the bottom right.

Beeps accompanying a countdown, a tap, and flashes from your iPhone let you know when to expect the shot.

Use HDR: Open the Camera app on your Apple Watch, firmly press the display, then tap HDR .

HDR (High Dynamic Range) helps you get great shots in high-contrast situations.

When shooting with HDR on, your iPhone takes multiple photos in rapid succession—at different exposure settings—and blends them together. The resulting photo has better detail in the bright and midtone areas.

Note: HDR is available with the rear-facing camera on an iPhone and the front-facing camera on the iPhone 5s and later.

Review Your Shots

Use the following actions to review your shots on your Apple Watch.

1. View a photo: Tap the thumbnail in the bottom left.

2. See other photos: Swipe left or right.

3. Zoom: Turn the Digital Crown.

4, Pan: Drag on a zoomed photo.

4. Fill the screen: Double-tap the screen.

5. Show or hide the Close button and the shot count: Tap the screen.

6. When you're finished, tap Close.

Chapter 21: View a Friend's Location With Apple Watch

You can find people who are so dear to you using the **Find My Friends** app. This is a great way to find people and share your location with them, especially if they use any Apple device.

You can use this app to get notifications when family members or friends arrive or leave various locations. To Add a person to your friends' list:

• Open the "**Find My Friends app"** on your iPhone.

• Tap Add, then choose a contact.

• Just Tap **Send** to send a request to a contact.

• When your friend agrees to give you their location, you can then see their location on a map in the "Find My Friends app.

To find out where they are

• On the Apple Watch, Open the Find My Friends app to view a list of your friends' location and distance from you.

• Then, Turn the Digital Crown to view more friends.

• If you Tap a friend, you will see their location on a map.

• Tap < icon in the top-left corner to go back to your friends' list

Return to friends list.

Scroll to get directions or send a message.

Get Notification about Your Friend's Location

You can also set to receive notifications of your friends' location.

To do this:

• Open the Find My Friends app on your Apple Watch.

• Then, Tap your friend,

• And scroll down,

• Then tap Notify Me and Turn on Notify Me,

160

- Then choose to receive notifications anytime your friends arrive at your location or leaves their location.

Notify a friend of your location;

- Open the Find My Friends app on your Apple Watch.

- Tap a friend,

- Tap Notify [name of friend].

- Then Turn on Notify [name of friend] on the next screen,

- After that select to notify your friend when you arrive at their location or leave your location.

See a Contact's Address on the Map

- Open the Maps app on your Apple Watch.

- And Tap Search,

- Then tap Contacts.

- After that, turn the Digital Crown to scroll,

- Then tap the address.

Find Places and Explore With Apple Watch

Your Apple Watch feature Maps app for getting directions or for exploring your surroundings.

Ask Siri. Say something like "Where am I?" "Find coffee near me."

- To Search the map; Open the Maps app on your Apple Watch.

- Tap Search,

- Then tap Dictation, then say what you're looking for.

Find nearby places,

- Open the Maps app on your Apple Watch.

162

- Tap Search

- Tap a category under Nearby,

- Then tap a category such as Shopping or food

- Tap a result,

- After that, turn the Digital Crown to scroll the information.

- Tap < sign in the top-left corner to return to the map.

Note that: not all nearby suggestions are available in all areas.

To See your surroundings and location

- Open the Maps app on your Apple Watch.

- Tap Location.

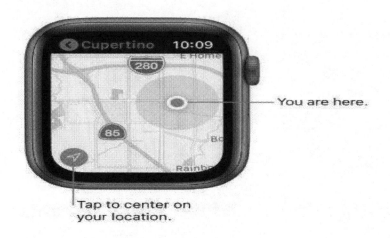

1. You can Pan the map by dragging it out with one finger.

2. Then Turn the Digital Crown to zoom the map in or out:

3. If you double-tap the map, it will zoom in on the spot you tap.

4. And to return to your current location, you want to tap the Location button at the bottom left.

5. If you want to get info about a marked location or landmark, tap the location marker on the map.

6. Then Turn the Digital Crown to scroll the info.

7. After that, Tap < sign in the top-left corner to go back to the map.

Other Tips to keep in mind;

• To call a location: Tap the Telephone number in the location info.

• To switch to your iPhone, unlock it, you have to tap the green bar at the top of the screen.

• To Drop a Map pin: Touch and hold the map to where you'd like the pin to go. Just wait for the pin to drop, then let go.

• To Move a pin just Drop a new pin in the new location.

• To delete a pin: Tap the Pin to see address information. Then turn the Digital Crown to scroll, and tap Remove Marker.

If you want the address of any spot on the map,

• Drop a pin on the location,

• And tap the pin to see address info.

How to Search For a Location in Maps

This is pretty straightforward

• Open Maps.

• Then Tap Search,

• Tap Dictation.

• Say what you're searching for, then tap done.

Turn Dictation on or off

OK, you are done with the recording and you want to turn it off or on Just head straight to the Settings > General > Keyboard. Turn Enable Dictation off or on.

Delete Conversation

On the conversation, swipe left.

• Tap the Trash icon

• Then Tap Trash again.

Chapter 22: Use Compass on Apple Watch

The compass icon tells you the bearing of your Apple Watch.

It also gives you an idea of your current location and elevation.

You will be able to see your bearings, elevation, incline, and coordinates. At the top left of your Apple Watch, you will be able to see your floor elevation, coordinates and incline when you scroll up.

1. Click on the Compass icon to open the app on your Apple Watch.

2. Make sure you align the crosshairs by placing the Apple Watch flat. This is for getting precise bearings.

3. Use the Digital Crown to make corrections on your bearing. Click 'Display' and press 'Edit Bearing' to find the Digital Crown.

You can set it to true north instead of using magnetic north. To do this: navigate to the settings app, press 'Compose' and then switch on the 'Use True North'

Keep in mind that some bands of Apple Watch are made of magnets which can affect the reading on the Compass.

Chapter 23: Create an emergency medical ID

A medical ID provides information about you that might be useful during an emergency situation like allergies and medical conditions. Your Apple Watch can display this information so that it's available for someone attending to you in an emergency.

Tip: Having an emergency medical ID that includes your date of birth is particularly important for those who are 65 and older.

Apple Watch Series 4 and later includes fall detection, which is turned on by default if you're 65 and older (it can be optionally turned on if you're under 65).

Set Up Your Medical ID

1. Open the Health app on your iPhone.

2, Tap your profile picture at the top right, then tap Medical ID.

3. Tap Get Started, then enter your information.

4. The Medical ID screen showing the user's name, date of birth, and age.

View your medical ID on Apple Watch

1. On your Apple Watch, hold the side button until the sliders appear.

2. Drag the Medical ID slider to the right.

If you don't see your medical ID when you hold the side button on your Apple Watch, open the Health app on your iPhone, tap your profile picture, tap Medical ID, tap Edit, then turn on Show When Locked. To hide your medical ID when your Apple Watch is locked, turn off Show When Locked.

Tip: Add emergency contacts to your medical ID, and your Apple Watch alerts them if you make an Emergency SOS call to emergency services.

How to Enable Fall Detection

The Apple Watch Series 5 has a built-in fall detection feature that will identify when it thinks you have fallen, and after a few seconds of no movement, will call emergency services on your behalf.

If the watch doesn't detect movement for "about a minute" after the fall, a 15-second countdown begins before it eventually calls emergency services. This also includes alerting your emergency contacts that you've fallen and you are no longer moving. If you'd like to enable fall detection, open the Watch app on your iPhone, then tap Emergency SOS.

Slide the switch next to Fall Detection to the On position. For users aged 65 or older who have entered their age during watch setup, or in the Health app, fall detection is automatically enabled. Apple states it is possible to accidentally trigger fall detection if you're highly active, particularly in high-impact activities.

So if you find yourself accidentally triggering fall detection, repeat the steps above to disable it.

Chapter 24: Chapter Cycle Tracking

As we earlier said in the introduction, the Apple Watch is made up of the new Cycle features to help **women** track their menstrual cycles. You can do this using the Cycle tracking app with tools to log various metrics and to get notifications about period and fertility.

Moreover, you can use the Cycle Tracking app, fill your menstrual cycle information.

You can attach data about the flow and keep track of signs like nausea or cramps.

The Cycle Tracking app will notify you once it foresees when your next period or fertile duration will begin. It uses the data you've logged in to do this.

Set up Cycle Tracking

1. Go to the Health app on your iPhone (specifically with iOS13 OS).

2. Click **'Browse'** which you will find at the lower right. This will bring out the Health Categories screen.

3. Click 'Cycle Tracking.'

4. Click **'Get Started.'** Afterward, follow the instructions on the screen to set alerts and other features.

5. Navigate to the page bottom > click 'Options', > switch on the options you

175

want (available options are Period Prediction and Fertility Prediction)

Log your cycle on Apple Watch

1. Go to the Cycle Tracking app from your watch.

2. And click the buttons and select features that explain your period (i.e. flow level and symptoms).

The remarks you give will show up in the iPhone Cycle Log. If you switched on Period Prediction and Fertility Prediction in the iPhone Health app, Apple Watch will notify you of future periods and fertility windows. The predictions given here cannot be used as a way to control births.

Chapter 25: Check Your Heart Rate on Apple Watch

Your heart rate is an important way to monitor how your body is doing. You can check your heart rate during a workout; see your resting, walking, breathe, workout, and recovery rates throughout the day; or take a new reading at any time.

The Heart Rate app screen, with your current heart rate showing in the bottom left, your last reading in smaller type below that, and a chart above detailing your heart rate throughout the day.

See Your Heart Rate

Open the Heart Rate app on your Apple Watch to view your current heart rate, resting rate, and walking average rate.

Your Apple Watch continues measuring your heart rate as long as you're wearing it.

Check Your Heart Rate During A Workout

By default, your current heart rate shows on the Multiple Metric workout view. To customize which metrics appear during a workout, follow these steps:

1. Open the Apple Watch app on your iPhone.

2. Tap My Watch, go to Workout > Workout View, then tap a workout.

Monitor your heart rate with a glance.

See a Graph of Your Heart Rate Data

1. Open the Health app on your iPhone.

2. Tap Browse at the bottom right, tap Heart, then tap Heart Rate.

3. To add Heart Rate to your Summary, swipe up, then tap Add to Favorites.

4. You can see your heart rate over the last hour, day, week, month, or year.

Tap Show All Filters and you can also see the range of your heart rate during the selected time period; your resting, walking average, workout, and breathe rates; and any high or low heart rate notifications.

Turn On Heart Rate Data

By default, your Apple Watch monitors your heart rate for the Heart Rate app, workouts, and Breathe sessions. If you've turned off heart rate data, you can turn it back on.

1. Open the Apple Watch app on your iPhone.

2. Tap My Watch, then tap Privacy.

3. Turn on Heart Rate.

Receive High Or Low Heart Rate Notifications

Your Apple Watch can notify you if your heart rate remains above a chosen threshold or below a chosen threshold after you've been inactive for at least 10 minutes.

You can turn on heart rate notifications when you first open the Heart Rate app, or at any time later.

1. Open the Apple Watch app on your iPhone.

2.Tap My Watch, then tap Heart.

3. Tap High Heart Rate, then choose a heart rate—120 bpm, for example.

4. Tap Low Heart Rate, then choose a heart rate—45 bpm, for example.

Receive irregular heart rhythm notifications (not available in all regions)

You can receive a notification if Apple Watch has identified an irregular heart rhythm that appears to be atrial fibrillation (AFib).

1. Open the Apple Watch app on your iPhone.

2. Tap My Watch, then tap Heart.

3. Tap Set Up Irregular Rhythm Notifications in Health, then follow the onscreen instructions.

Note: For best results, the back of your Apple Watch needs skin contact for features like wrist detection, haptic notifications, and the heart rate sensor. Wearing your Apple Watch with the right fit—not too tight, not too loose, and with room for your skin to breathe—keeps you comfortable and lets the sensors do their job. You may want to tighten your Apple Watch for workouts, then loosen the band when you're done. Water may prevent, or reduce the accuracy of heart rate monitoring.

In addition, the sensors work only when you wear your Apple Watch on the top of your wrist.

Chapter 26: Hearing Health— Measure Noise Levels With Apple Watch

The Series 5 Apple Watch uses the speaker and screen interval to estimate the background noise concentrations in your surroundings.

The app which can be found in Series 5 can alert you with a click on the wrist when it detects that the noise level has increased to a stage where hearing might be impaired.

Note: The Noise app samples and estimates the sound concentrations in your setting using the speaker. There is no recordings done in this process.

Set up the Noise App

1. Open your Apple Watch's Noise app.

2. Click **'Enable'** to start monitoring the environment.

3. Open the Noise app or use the Noise complication to assess noise in your surrounding

Get Noise Notifications

1. Open your iPhone's Apple Watch.

2. Click 'My Watch' and click 'Noise'.

4. Under 'Noise Notifications',

5. Click 'Noise Threshold', then select a configuration.

View information about environmental sound levels

1. Navigate to the Health app on your iPhone.

2. Press 'Browse', and tap 'Hearing', then Press 'Environmental Sound Levels'.

Turn off noise measuring

1. Go to the Settings app on your Apple Watch.

2. Navigate to Noise>Environmental Sound Measurements.

3. Switch off 'Measure Sounds.'

It is possible to switch the noise estimation from your iPhone.

Go to the Apple Watch app on your iPhone > Click 'My Watch > click 'Noise' > Switch off 'Environmental Sound Measurements.'

Chapter 27: Control Your Home with Apple Watch

Yes, you can use the Apple Watch Home App to turn on a light quickly, set the thermostat, control a switch, or lock the door. If you Ask Siri and Say something like: "Turn off the lights in the office."

Add a New Scene or Accessory to the Home App

You can Use the Home app on your iPhone to create a new scene or accessory.

You will see that your favorite accessories and scenes are on your Apple Watch.

If you want to set an item as a favorite,

- Head over to the Home app on your iPhone

- Tap Rooms.

- Swipe right or left to find the scene or accessory.

- Then touch and hold it.

- Tap Settings, and turn on "Include in Favorites."

When you have added a new accessory or scene to your favorites, it will then show up in the Home app on your Apple Watch.

Raise to Speak to Siri

On your new Apple Watch series 5, you don't have to press the Digital Crown or say "Hey Siri" to speak to Siri.

Now, you need to "lift your arm, move it closer to your face, and start speaking. With Siri

Siri will instantly identity and start transcribing your commands.

Personally, I've found this method to be way faster than other methods of communicating to Siri on the Apple Watch. And it actually makes Siri useful on the wrist!

Control Smart Home Accessories and Scenes

To control a scene,

- On the Apple Watch, open the Home app

- Then tap a scene to turn it on or off.

- If you have multiple home set up, you want to choose which one to view on your Apple Watch.

- Then, Open the Home app on your Apple Watch.

- And Firmly press the display,

- Then tap Change Home.

- Finally, Tap the home you want to see.

Remotely Access Your Smart Home Appliances From Apple Watch

If you have an Apple TV (3rd generation or later), HomePod, or an iPad (iPadOS 13 or iOS 10 or later) that you leave at home, you can remotely access HomeKit-enabled accessories from your iPhone and your paired Apple Watch. The Apple TV, HomePod, or iPad acts as a home hub that lets you communicate with your accessories when you're away from home.

Allow Remote Access

On your iPhone, go to Settings > [your name] > iCloud, then turn on Home. Make sure you're signed in using the same Apple ID on all the devices.

If you have an Apple TV and you're signed in using the same Apple ID as your iPhone, it will be paired automatically.

Chapter 28: How to Read and Reply Messages on Apple Watch

Apple Watch allows you to have a gentle tap to let you see any new messages on your Apple Watch.

Read a message

• Press the Digital Crown to view all your message apps,

• Then tap the Messages app or open the Messages from the Dock.

• If you get a notification about a message, just raise your wrist to view it or swipe down on the watch face to see the message.

Reply to a Message

To reply a message,

• Scroll to the end of the message,

• Then choose an option.

• You can send a preset reply, or use Scribble, or record a response, and more

• If you want to use preset replies,

• You will have to scroll down to the end of the message, and then tap a reply. You can also choose the way you want to reply.

- If you want to reply to the person by sending an emoji, tap the emoji icon.

- If you want to send a handwritten message or sticker, Tap emoji icon, scroll down,

- Then tap Stickers to use a different sticker, or message, utilize Messages on your iPhone.

- If you'd like to record a message, tap the Microphone icon to record something. After that, tap Send or Done.

How to Use Scribble on your Apple Watch

The Scribble feature allows you to write with your finger, rather than to use a keyboard.

Meaning, you can write on your watch's screen, and, your Apple watch turns your writing into text.

You can use this feature to reply to a message or an email.

To go about this;

• Tap Scribble, and write a word in the text box.

• Or enter any letters, punctuation, and numbers. You'd need to turn the Digital Crown to choose predictive text.

Send a New Message

Siri can help you create a new message if you ask her. For instance, ask Siri to "Tell Jack I won't be coming to the party."

- After that lower your wrist to send. Apart from asking Siri, follow these alternate steps

- Open the home screen by pressing the Digital Crown

- Then tap the Messages app.

- Press the display firmly and tap New Message.

- Then Tap Add Contact.

- Tap any contact in the list that shows up,

- Then tap the Contact button to see more contacts,

- After that, tap the Microphone button to look for someone.

• You can as well dictate a phone number, or better still tap the Keypad button to fill in a phone number.

Create your message

If you would like to add some styles to your text, here's how to customize a reply:

• On your iPhone, open the Apple Watch app

• Tap the My Watch tab.

• Go to Messages and then Default Replies.

• Then change it by tapping a default reply.

• If you want to delete a default reply or change the order, tap Edit.

Use Dictation on your Apple Watch

The Apple Watch gives you the option to use your voice, known as Dictation to reply to messages and email.

The best part is that you can use it for other minor tasks, like searching for Maps. So, how do we explore this nice feature?

• To reply to a message using dictation, open the message.

• Then Scroll to the bottom, and tap microphone icon.

• Record your message. Ensure you say punctuation or full stop or question mark" to where you want it to be.

• Then Tap Send when you're done recording.

- To send the message as text instead of audio;

- Change the setting on your iPhone.

- Then Open the Apple Watch app,

- And tap the My Watch Tab.

- Tap Messages

•Then tap dictate messages to send dictated message.

Reply to an Email

- To reply to an email, Fire up the email and tap reply at the end of the message.

• You can also press the screen firmly and tap Reply

• Then Tap the microphone icon.

• Record your message and then tap done.

- Ensure you say punctuation. For example, say "How was the event question mark?"

• After that, check your message, and tap Send.

Choose which mailboxes appear on Apple Watch

1. Open the Apple Watch app on your iPhone.

2. Tap My Watch, then go to Mail > Include Mail.

3. Tap the accounts you want to see on your Apple Watch under Accounts. You can specify multiple accounts—for example, iCloud and the account you use at work.

4. If you want, tap an account, then tap specific mailboxes to see their contents on your Apple Watch.

By default you see messages from all inboxes. You can also choose to view messages from VIPs, flagged messages, unread messages, and more.

You can also choose the accounts and mailboxes you see, right on Apple Watch. Open the Mail app , scroll down, tap Edit, then tap an account or mailbox.

View specific accounts on Apple Watch

Open the Mail app on your Apple Watch.

1. Tap < in the top-left corner to see a list of accounts and special mailboxes, such as Flagged and Unread.

2. Tap an account or mailbox to view its contents.

3. To see your email from all accounts, tap All Inboxes.

4. Delete, mark as unread or read, or flag a message

5. Open the Mail app on your Apple Watch, tap the message, then firmly press the display to:

6. Delete a message: Tap Trash.

If you're looking at the message list, swipe left on the message, then tap the Trash button.

Mark a message unread or read: Tap Unread or Read.

If you're looking at the message list, swipe right on the message, then tap the Read or Unread button.

Flag a message: Tap Flag. (You can also unflag a message that's already been flagged.)

If you're looking at the message list, swipe left on the message, then tap the Flag button.

To change the flag style, open the Apple Watch app on your iPhone, tap My Watch, then go to Mail > Custom > Flag Style.

When you press the display while viewing a message on Apple Watch, four buttons appear on the screen: Reply, Flag, Unread, and Trash.

If you swipe on a message thread, the action you choose (Trash, Flag, Read, or Unread) applies to the entire thread.

Customize Alerts

1. Open the Apple Watch app on your iPhone.

2. Tap My Watch, go to Mail > Custom, tap an account, then turn on Show Alerts.

3. Turn Sound and Haptic on or off.

Shorten Your Message List

To make your mail list more compact, reduce the number of preview text lines shown for each email in the list.

1. Open the Apple Watch app on your iPhone.

2. Tap My Watch, tap Mail, then tap Message Preview.

3. Choose to show only 1 line, or none.

Load Remote Images

Some emails can contain links that point to online images. If you allow remote images to load, those images appear in the email. To allow these images, follow these steps:

1. Open the Apple Watch app on your iPhone.

2. Tap My Watch, tap Mail, tap Custom, then turn on Load Remote Images.

Note: Loading remote images can cause email to download more slowly to your Apple Watch.

Chapter 29: Listen to Music on Apple Watch and other Audio

Use the Music app to choose and play music on Apple Watch. Subscribe to and use the Music app to control, play and stream music on Apple Watch.

Ask Siri:

- "Play more songs from this album"
- "Play my Training/workout playlist"

Play music

Tap for more options.

Open the Music app on your Apple Watch (that's after pairing Bluetooth speakers or headphones). After that, you can:

1. Play music on your Apple Watch by turning the Digital Crown to scroll through album artwork, before tapping an album or playlist it.

Use the Apple Watch app on your iPhone to choose which songs to add to Apple Watch.

2. You can play music from your iPhone (without Bluetooth pairing) by scrolling to the top of the screen, tapping On iPhone, before tapping a playlist, artist, album, or song to play it.

3. You could also play music from your music library by tapping Library before

tapping an album, playlist, or song that is not on your Apple Watch to play it.

4. To listen to Apple Music (you must have an active Apple Music subscription) by raising your wrist, then requesting the artist, album, song, or genre of music you want.

Turn the Digital Crown to browse more music.

Play Music for You

You can play curated music if you're an Apple Music subscriber.

Here's how:

1. Simply open the Music app on your Apple Watch.

2. Then scroll to the top of the screen after which you tap **For You i**n order to check out the curated feed of playlists and albums based on your tastes

3. Just tap an album or playlist, then tap the Play button and the music plays.

Open the Up Next Queue

You can view a list of upcoming songs in the Up Next queue while playing music:

1. Simply open the Music app on your Apple Watch.

2. Then play an album or playlist before tapping the Up Next Queue button.

3. You then tap any song you want to be played, to listen to it.

If you want to add music to the queue simply swipe left on a song, playlist, or album. Next, you tap the More button before tapping Play Next or Play Later(these songs are sent to the end of the queue).

How to Tell Music what you like, and also add music to the library

With your Apple Watch, you get to do so much; add music to your library; remove songs; select what you like or not; add songs to the Up Next queue and view the contents of albums and playlists. Here's how:

- Check out the options from the Now Playing screen while playing music.

You then tap the More button to choose an option.

- Take a look at the options in **For You and Library.** You then swipe left on a song, playlist, or album, tap the More button before choosing an option.

Control playback

You can play music on your Apple Watch and iPhone by using these controls:

▶	Play the current song.
❚❚	Pause playback.
▶▶	Skip to the next song.
◀◀	Skip to the beginning of the song; double-tap to skip to the previous song.

Shuffle or repeat music

- You can shuffle albums, songs, artists, from the Music screen by tapping an album, artist, or playlist before tapping the Shuffle button.

- You can also shuffle or repeat music from the playback screen by tapping the Up Next Queue button before tapping the Shuffle or Repeat buttons.

Better still, just tap Repeat twice to repeat a song.

Listen to Music without IPhone

You can listen to music in your Apple Watch, even without your iPhone with you. To do this:

- You will have to choose which playlists are added automatically to Apple Watch.

- Open the Apple Watch app on your iPhone.

- Tap on My Watch,

- Then tap on Music.

If you subscribe to Apple Music, then the Favorites Mix and New Music Mix playlists are added automatically to your Apple Watch when it's connected to power. You still turn off any playlists you do not wish to add.

Both Apple Music non-subscribers and subscribers can also decide to add Heavy Rotation to their Apple Watch.

In case you don't know, Heavy Rotation is a collection of playlists and album you select based on your iPhone listening habits.

To add albums and playlists to Apple Watch:

- On your iPhone, open the Apple Watch app.

- Tap My Watch, and tap Music.

- Then Under Playlists & Albums, tap Add Music.

- Choose albums and playlists so you can add them to your Apple Watch.

You can also Use the Music app on your iPhone to create playlists specifically for music you feel like listening to on your Apple Watch.

For example, if you want to listen to music that motivates you during a workout:

- Add a workout playlist to Watch

- Then open the Apple Watch app on your iPhone.

- Tap My Watch, and then tap Workout.

- The next step is to Tap the Workout Playlist, and choose a playlist. The playlist will automatically start playing when you start a workout except you're currently listening to another audio or music.

You can also view how much music has been stored on your Apple Watch by:

- Opening the Settings app on your Apple Watch.

- Head over to General

- From there to About,

- Then look under Songs. You will be able to see how much music has been stored on your Apple Watch.

Add Music to Apple Watch

Apple Watch comes with a couple of GBS free. You have the option to load it up with your favorite music to allow it to be there with you. Open the Watch app on your iPhone and head to the Music section.

If you've enabled the feature, it will automatically add playlists like heavy rotation, favorites and more.

But you can add any album or playlist you want. Tap on the Add Music button and choose the album.

The music is automatically downloaded to the Apple Watch when it's charging and is near the iPhone.

If you have a cellular Apple Watch, you can stream any song from Apple Music no matter where you are.

Use the Apple Watch app on your iPhone to adjust settings, customize watch faces, and configure the Dock, notifications, install apps, and more.

- Open the Apple Watch app on your iPhone

- Then tap the Apple Watch app icon.

• Tap My Watch to see the settings for your Apple Watch.

If you have multiple Apple Watch paired with your iPhone, you'll see the settings for your active Apple Watch.

Swipe to see your watch face collection.

Settings for Apple Watch.

Remove Music from Apple Watch

● To do this, Open the Apple Watch app on your iPhone.

● Tap My Watch, and then tap Music.

● Then Turn off any playlists you do not desire on your Apple Watch.

If you want to delete albums and playlists you've added to your Apple Watch,

● Tap Edit,

● Then tap the Delete button next to the items you want to remove

● Note that the Music you delete from your Apple Watch is still in your iPhone.

Chapter 30: Listen to radio on Apple Watch

Radio is the home of Beats 1, which features world-class radio shows, the latest music, and exclusive interviews. You can also listen to featured stations that have been crafted by music experts, and broadcast radio.

Listen to Beats 1

To listen to Beats 1, make sure your Apple Watch is near your iPhone or connected to a Wi-Fi network—or a cellular network, if you have an Apple Watch with cellular.

1. Open the Radio app on your Apple Watch.

2. Turn the Digital Crown to scroll to the top of the screen.

Tap Stations, then tap the currently playing Beats 1 show.

Listen To A Featured Or Genre Station

You must be an Apple Music subscriber to listen to featured or genre stations.

1. Open the Radio app on your Apple Watch.

2. Tap Stations, then turn the Digital Crown to scroll through stations and genres created by music experts.

3. Tap a genre to see its stations.

4. Tap a station to play it.

5. Listen to broadcast radio

You can listen to thousands of broadcast radio stations on your Apple Watch.

Ask Siri. Say something like "Play Wild 94.9" or "Tune in to ESPN Radio."

You can ask for stations by name, call sign, frequency, and nickname.

Note: You don't need a subscription to Apple Music to listen to broadcast radio.

Broadcast radio isn't available in all countries or regions. Not all stations are available in all countries or regions.

Listen To Radio Over a Cellular Connection

To listen to radio over cellular, you must be using Apple Watch with cellular.

1. On your iPhone go to Settings > Music.

2. Tap Cellular Data, then turn on Streaming.

3. Add and rate songs

If you're an Apple Music subscriber, you can add the currently playing song to your library as well as rate it.

4. Open the Radio app on your Apple Watch.

5. Tap Stations, then tap a station.

6. Tap the More button, then tap Add to Library,   Love, or Suggest Less.

To view the album a song comes from, tap View Album to open the album in the Music app.

Chapter 31: How to Use the Podcasts App on Apple Watch

You can now enjoy the podcast feature in Apple Watch series 5 when you're on the go.

This podcast feature enables you to sync your favorite iOS Podcasts on both your Apple Watch and iPhone.

Unfortunately, Apple didn't give direct instructions on how to set up the podcasts on Apple Watch.

• To begin with, install the Apple Podcasts app on both devices.

• Ensure you pair a Bluetooth speaker or headphones to your Apple Watch to listen to the podcasts since you can't listen to podcasts without connecting to an audio device.

How to Install Podcast Episodes on Apple Watch

Any Podcasts you save in the built-in Podcast app will automatically move from your iPhone to your Apple Watch when you're charging your Apple Watch.

You can listen to podcasts from your Apple Watch via LTE, Wi-Fi, based on your WiFi model (Wi-Fi only or Wi-Fi + LTE). Note that after each episode play, they will be deleted from the device automatically.

How to customize the Podcast Experience on Apple Watch

Storage, especially on Apple Watch, is a precious commodity.

Therefore, I'd suggest limiting the number of podcasts you store on the device. To do so, you have to make changes in the Apple Watch app for iPhone.

How to Use the Podcasts App on Apple Watch Series 5

The Podcasts app on Apple Watch looks familiar with the Music app. To use it:

• Press the Digital Crown on your Apple Watch to select the Home screen. And Tap the Podcasts app.

- On the main screen, you'll see links for "On iPhone, Now Playing, and Library".

- Tap On iPhone to view podcasts on your phone but not necessarily installed on the watch.

- **"Listen Now"** is where you'll find a link to the latest episode of each podcast you follow.

- Under **Shows** are links to your subscribed podcasts.

- Tap to see a running list of all episodes in the series.

- With "Episodes," you'll find all the available episodes, sorted by newest to oldest, regardless of the podcast.

- Stations give you access to groups of podcasts; you create stations from the Podcasts app on iPhone.

- Tap **Now playing** to see the most recent podcast that played on your Apple Watch. It includes the same controls you can find in the Music app.

- Tap **Library** to see a list of unplayed episode titles organized by release date. There is also a list showing each podcast title. If you click on any of these links, they will show the episodes available on Apple Watch.

Note: Library is where you'll find episodes downloaded to your Apple Watch.

These episodes are available even when your Apple Watch isn't connected to Wi-Fi or LTE.

Chapter 32: Listen To Audiobooks

As we all know, Apple has integrated a new Audiobook app which allows you to listen to audiobooks directly from the watch on your wrist unlike before when you will need to start the audiobook on your iPhone before getting access.

The titles of your Apple books that are available on your Reading Now list will automatically get synced to your watch.

Play audiobooks stored on Apple Watch

1. First, connect a Bluetooth headphone.

2. Navigate to the Audiobooks app on your series 5 watch.

3. Switch on the Digital Crown in order to scroll through the Audiobook options.

4. Press the Audiobook you want to play

5. Play audiobooks on iPhone

6. Navigate to the Audiobook app from your Apple Watch

7. Click on iPhone

8. Press the Audiobook you want to play

9. Play audiobooks from your library

It is possible to stream audiobooks from its store to your Apple Watch. This is possible if the watch is close to your iPhone device or connected with Wi-Fi. It is also possible with cellular network if the watch model uses cellular.

1. From your Apple Watch, Go to the Audiobooks app.

2. Press 'Library' and click on the Audiobook you want to **play.**

3. Play audiobooks with Siri

4. Tell Siri what audiobook to play from your library selection

5. "Play the audiobook 'Where the Crawdads Sing.'"

Control playback

Use the following controls for audiobook playback:

▶	Play the audiobool
❚❚	Pause playback.
(15)↻	Skip ahead 15 sec
(15)↺	Skip back 15 seco
1×	Playback speed. O 1/4x, 1 1/2x, 1 3/4x
☰	Choose a track or

Chapter 33: Voice Memos

You can use the Voice Memos app on your Apple Watch to record personal notes. Here's how

Record a voice memo

1. Start by opening the Voice Memos app on your Apple Watch.

2. You then tap the Record button.

3. To stop the recording, just tap the Stop Recording button.

Here's How To Play A Voice Memo

1. Just open the Voice Memos app on your Apple Watch.

2. Then tap a recording on the Voice Memos screen, before tapping the Play button to play it.

3. All you need to do to delete the recording is tap the More button before tapping Delete.

Always remember that those voice memos you record on your Apple Watch are automatically synchronized to your iOS devices signed in with the same Apple ID.

Chapter 34: Connect Apple Watch to Bluetooth headphones or speakers

Play audio from Apple Watch on Bluetooth headphones or speakers without your iPhone nearby.

Tip: If you have AirPods that you set up with your iPhone, they're ready to use with your Apple Watch—just press play.

Pair Bluetooth Headphones or Speakers

You need Bluetooth headphones or speakers to listen to most audio on your Apple Watch (voice memos play through the speaker on Apple Watch).

Follow the instructions that came with the headphones or speakers to put them in discovery mode. When the Bluetooth device is ready, follow these steps:

1. Open the Settings app on your Apple Watch, then tap Bluetooth.

2. Tap the device when it appears.

You can also tap the AirPlay button on the play screens of the Audiobooks, Music, Now Playing, Podcasts, and Radio apps to open the Bluetooth setting.

Choose An audio Output

Touch and hold the bottom of the screen, then swipe up to open Control Center. Tap the Audio Output icon, then choose the device you want to use.

Chapter 35: Setting up the Walkie-Talkie

As part of the recent update, Apple also included a new toggle in the Control Center for turning the Walkie-Talkie feature on and off.

This now makes it easier to have a one-on-one conversation with anyone who owns a compatible Apple Watch.

The walkie-talkie toggle is located right from within the control center.

• All you need do is to swipe up through the control center

• From there you will see the walkie-talkie toggle.

If you press it, then it will show whether you're online or offline inside the walkie talking app.

This way, you don't have to jump into the app, and you don't need to waste complications to get there.

And once you get there with this method, the next step is to add a friend you want to chat with.

To do that:

- Open the Walkie-Talkie app.

- Turn on the Digital Crown to let you scroll through your contacts.

- Then choose a friend who owns an Apple Watch and WatchOS 5.

- Tap on the friend's name in the contacts list.

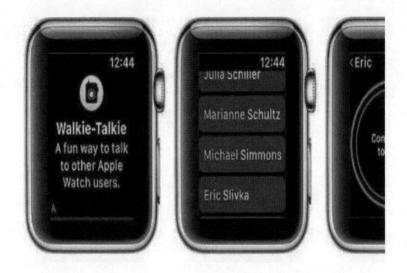

- You will see a yellow card while your friend's name appears on your Apple Watch in the Walkie-Talkie app,

- Tap on the card.

- Then Press on the "Talk" button to carry out a connection.

- After that, wait for your friend to get and approve your message from the Walkie-Talkie connection. It will say "Connecting to [Your Friend's Name]."

- When it finally connects, it will go back to the Talk button, and you will have a fluid Walkie-Talkie conversation with your friend.

If there's a failure in connection, then you will see a popup that says "[Your Friend] is not available." That means, your friend did not answer the incoming Walkie-Talkie notification from his end.

Also, if the Walkie-Talkie connection screen hangs while connecting the screen, it means your friend does not own an Apple Watch or has the watchOS 5 installed.

What about if a friend adds you to Walkie-Talkie?

Then you'll see an incoming notification from your friend, who wants to create a connection with you. To chat with him or her, you will need to tap on **"Always Allow."**

And once a connection has been established,

• Open up the Walkie-Talkie app.

•   Then tap on the card for the person you'd like to talk to.

•   Hold the "Talk" button down for the whole time you'd be speaking.

• Then a little concentric circle will show up that your message is sent to your friend.

• Stop Pressing the "Talk button" when you're done. This will let your friend reply the message by pressing the Talk button on their end.

Adjusting Walkie-Talkie Volume

You can easily adjust the Walkie-Talkie volume by following these steps:

- Open the Walkie-Talkie app.

- Select a Walkie-Talkie contact card.

- Turn the Digital Crown at the talking interface.

- If you turn it downward, it will lower the Walkie-Talkie volume

- While an upward turn will make it louder.

Turning Off Walkie-Talkie and Removing Contacts

You can turn off Walkie-Talkie conversations and stop incoming messages.

To do this:

- Open up the Walkie-Talkie app.

- Scroll to the top to see the "Available" toggle.

- Then toggle "Available" to off.

If you disable the Walkie-Talkie availability in the Walkie-Talkie app, people who want to connect to you will see the message as "[Your Name] is Not Available."

But you will still get the notification that someone tried to reach out to you, but you were unavailable. You will also see the option to resume the conversation in the Walkie-Talkie app. If you want to remove a contact from Walkie-Talkie, then: Swipe to the left at the name in the list contact card interface to bring up a red "X" button. And Press on the X to delete the contact.

Chapter 36: Update Your Height and Weight

The Apple Watch can help you enjoy a more healthy life in a variety of ways. Just ensure your personal info is up to date

- In your watch, go to the iPhone section, from there go to My Watch

- Then to Health

- Next, Edit.

So how do you update your height and weight on Apple Watch?

1. Click the Apple Watch app on your iPhone.

2. Select My Watch, scroll to Health > Health Profile, thereafter click Edit.

3. Hit Weight or Height, inputting your preferences.

The data you provide for variables like; weight, height, age, gender, and disability status on Apple Watch creates a pattern that determines the number of calories expended.

This includes the miles that you have covered and a host of other pertinent details when you are engaged in aerobic activities.

It gets to a point where, from constant use, the Workout application knows your performance and keeps tab on your fitness as you constantly test your endurance, including the calories used up.

Using IPhone GPS allows your Apple Watch to achieve even more distance accuracy.

For example, if you carry your iPhone while using the Workout app on a run, your Apple Watch uses the iPhone GPS to calibrate your stride.

Then later, if you're not carrying your iPhone, or if you're working out where GPS is unavailable (for example, indoors), your Apple Watch uses the data on your stride to measure distance and creates a pattern of performance.

Similarly, Apple Watch may use the built-in GPS to calibrate your movement. Your workout view can be altered when you;

1. Open the Apple Watch app on your iPhone.

2. Tap My Watch and swipe up to Workout > Workout View

3. Select Multiple Metric or Single Metric.

Have in mind that ternary Metric gives you binary results on a single interface.

Subsequently, in order to see other options and select the kind of results for your workout preference, for instance, during your walking and mountaineering activity, you may want to know how fast you climbed a trail or simply know the distance you have covered above ground level, do the following;

4. Click the workout type

5. Tap Edit to subsequently delete or add metrics and reorder by sweeping up.

When you are engaged in your routines, select another indicator like temperature or heart rate by switching the Digital Crown. When you are done with creating and adjusting settings, suspend your sessions automatically with the following steps;

6. Open Apple Watch Settings

7. Select Workout,

8. Enable Running Auto Pause.

Enable or Disable Workout Alerts

Your Apple Watch responds to the movement of your muscles and signals as soon as you start using the Workout application. Similarly, when you are in the middle of a session and need a breather to rest a little bit, the application notifies you to put your exercise on hold and grants you sweet rewards for completed sessions.

1. Open the Settings app on your Apple Watch.

2. Open Workout,

Change the Start Workout Reminder

End Workout Reminder settings. (Workout notices are enabled by default.)

To achieve the same objective in another convenient way;

1. Go to Apple Watch app on your iPhone, Lightly touch My Watch, stroke Workout,

2. Change the workout reminder settings.

Avoid unintended taps

Sometimes, locking your IPhone is the best option to disallow your workout from being disrupted often caused by your clothing gear. You can take the following actions;

Lock the screen: Scroll to the right and stroke Lock.

Ignore a notification: Enable the Digital Crown.

Unlock screen: Turn Digital Crown.

Economize power during a workout

You can preserve power at the cost of getting calories-expended results which is invariably inaccurate when you are out there on the trail, jogging and hiking.

In addition, you may need to switch off the heart rate indicator, as it consumes more battery life than other metrics.

Click the Settings icon on your Apple Watch. Go to Workout and Enable power saving mode.

Chapter 37: How to Use Your Apple Watch as a Waterproof Device

Did you know that using your Apple Watch series 5 gadgets at the pool or in the bath is now possible? So, that means you don't need to take your watch off if you want to swim or take a shower, as the watch is specifically designed for swimming.

This particular model features an ISO rating of 22810:2010 to help withstand water up to 50 meters (164 feet) of depth.

While this may be true, Apple still frowns against the act of water sking or scuba diving with the watch on your wrist.

In fact, Apple warns against anything that can force water into ports of the watch at high depths or high speed.

Of course, you can wear the watch in fresh or ocean water but always keep in mind to rinse off your watch with fresh water after swimming in the ocean to expel any salt. To be more protective, always activate Water Lock on the Apple Watch anytime you're swimming.

The Water Lock feature will keep water from activating the touchscreen of your watch. Note: If you start a Pool Swim or Open Water Swim Exercise Activity in your Apple Watch, then you have automatically enabled the Water Lock Feature.

Or, you can quickly activate Water Lock in Control Center by swiping up on the watch face and tapping on the water icon.

To disable Water Lock: Turn the Digital Crown on your watch until it brings up beeps sound. The noise the speaker emits is used to remove any water inside the cavity. While all these are true, we do NOT recommend wearing your Apple Watch in the shower, even though they are made to withstand fresh water.

The reason is that such practices can put out high-velocity of water, and the chemicals from soaps and shampoos can deteriorate the watch.

Chapter 38: How to set up Apple Pay on Apple Watch

One of the key benefits of the Apple Watch is that it allows everyone around the globe to use Apple Pay to buy things from the wrist.

Isn't that amazing?!!

The good news is that it's pretty easy to set up and use. So, how do you set it up and use them to shop for items?

How to Set Up and Use Apple Pay on Your Apple Watch

To set up your Apple Pay, you need an Apple ID. You also need an Apple ID to sign into iCloud and to have the passcode feature turned on in your watch.

This will prevent someone from using your card when you lost your watch.

Also, when you're using Apple Pay on your phone, you need to add a card to your watch.

Don't worry.

Your card is safe, since the credit card's information is never stored on your phone or transferred to a merchant.

So, here is how you set it up:

• On your iPhone, go to the watch app and tap on it.

• Then scroll down to wallet and Apple pay and tap on it.

• After that, you will see the cards you have entered on your phone.

• If you look down a little bit, you will see other areas that show other cards on your phone.

• So, take your card you already have on your phone and add it to your watch by tapping add, close to the card details.

• It will prompt you to use a credit card security code, put that in and tap up in the upper right

• It will bring up the terms and conditions. Then tap agree.

• Wait for a few seconds for it to load.

• Then go back to your wallet and Pay area, you will see that your card info is already loaded.

• If you scroll down, you will see the option to customize notifications.

• Once you're through with that, Go to the Apple watch and tap on the digital crown.

It will take you to the Apple Page where you're going to navigate around and tap on The Apple Pay app.

• Then it will bring up your card details, ready to shop.

How to Use your Apple Watch

When you're in the grocery store, and you have bought all your items, and you want to pay, what you need to do is to bring up your Apple watch. Double click the side button to bring up Apple pay. You can use the default card or swipe for another one.

Chapter 39: Use reward cards on Apple Watch

If you have a rewards card from a supporting merchant, you can add it to Wallet, then present it to a contactless reader as part of your transaction using your Apple Watch.

Add a rewards card to Apple Watch

Adding a rewards card from your email or a website link from your iPhone notification is possible using these sets of actions;

1. Look for an "Add to Apple Wallet" link.
2. Swipe the link to add the rewards card to Wallet.

When you allow this function, you can start using reward points from website links and email. However, on the notification panel, do the following;

1. Make payments with Apple Pay while providing your reward card data.

2. On the receipt of a notification, add the card as rewards card

3. Swipe up the notification while clicking Add

Use a rewards card on Apple Watch

When you're prompted to provide your rewards information while the Apple Pay logo is boldly presented, follow these steps:

1. Double-click the side button.

2. Swipe to select your preferred payment card.

3. Point your Apple Watch at an arm's length to the digital reader, the interface directly looking at the reader.

4. Use your rewards card without paying using Apple Pay

5. Double-click the side button.

6. Swipe to the rewards card.

7. Hold your Apple Watch to the reader, the interface directly looking at the digital reader.

Chapter 40: Pay with Apple Watch on Mac

When you surf websites that allows Apple Pay,

1. Initiate the purchase on your Mac using Safari browser, concluding the transaction on Apple Watch.

2. If you want to know the status of your transaction on Apple Watch, sign in to iCloud using Apple ID on your Mac and IPhone.

3. In addition, Your Mac and Apple Watch should be placed beside each other, with a Wi-Fi access.

Shop on your Mac and pay on Apple Watch

If you are buying stuff online using a Mac with Safari browser,

1. Select the Apple Pay option during checkout.
2. Review the payment, shipping, and billing information on your Mac, ascertaining this "Confirm with Apple Watch" Feedback.
3. Stroke the side button twice to purchase using your Apple Watch.
4. Choose your card preference that is attached to your Apple Watch.

Turn off Apple Pay payments on Mac

By default, you can use your Apple Watch to confirm Apple Pay payments made on your Mac.

If you don't want to confirm payments with your Apple Watch, follow these steps:

1. Open the Apple Watch app on your iPhone.
2. Tap My Watch,
3. Swipe to Wallet & Apple Pay,
4. Disable Allow Payments on Mac.

Chapter 41: Check the weather on Apple Watch

You can check reports on your Apple Watch by asking siri to do that for you.

For example, Siri "What's tomorrow's forecast for Honolulu?"

You can also check the current conditions and temperature for the day in your Apple Watch.

To do that:

• Open the Weather app on your Apple Watch.

• You will see hourly conditions; UV index, air quality and wind speed information. You will also see a 10-day forecast on a weather report.

When you Tap a city, scroll down.

- Then Tap < icon on the top-left corner, so you can return to the list of cities.

1. To view more weather, Open the weather app on your Apple Watch.
2. Then tap city.

3. Firmly press on the display, and tap to view hourly forecasts of, conditions, rains or temperature.

If you want to cycle through this forecast, you can also tap the display.

Turn to see details for other cities.

Press to see temperature or precipitation forecast.

Swipe left to see 10-day forecast.

How to Add a City

To add any city of your choice, on your Apple watch, open the Weather app.

- Scroll down to the bottom of the list of cities.
- Then tap Add City.
- Tap Scribble, or Dictation
- Thereafter, enter the city's name.
- Tap done, and tap the name of the city in the list results.

How to Remove a City

To remove a city,

- On your Apple Watch, Open the Weather app
- Tap the city you'd like to remove.
- Press the display firmly, then tap Remove.
- This will remove the city from Apple Watch and iPhone.

Choose your default city

To choose your default city,

- Open the Apple Watch app on your iPhone.
- Tap on My Watch
- Then go to Weather
- And then to Default City.

Your Apple Watch will show the weather conditions for that city on the watch face, whenever you add weather to the face.

Chapter 42: Adjust Brightness, Sounds, Text Sizes and Haptics on Apple Watch

You can easily adjust the brightness and text on your Apple watch if you:

- Open the Settings app on your Apple Watch, and tap Brightness & Text Size to do the following:

Brightness: To adjust brightness, tap the Brightness controls to adjust. Or tap the slider, and turn the Digital Crown.

Text size:

- To adjust text size, tap the text size and tap the letters or turn the digital crown to adjust the size.

You want to bold the text size?

- Turn Bold Text on.

If you want to make these adjustments on your iPhone, instead of the Watch:

- Open the Apple Watch app on your iPhone,
- Tap My Watch,
- Then tap Brightness & Text Size,
- After that, adjust the brightness and text.

Adjust Sound

To adjust the sound settings open the settings app on your Apple Watch.

- Tap Sounds & Haptics.
- Then under Alert Volume, Tap the volume controls or tap the slider.
- Then turn the Digital Crown to adjust.

You can do this also on your iPhone, by opening the Apple Watch app, and tap Sounds & Haptics. Then ensure you drag the Alert Volume slider.

Adjust Haptic Intensity

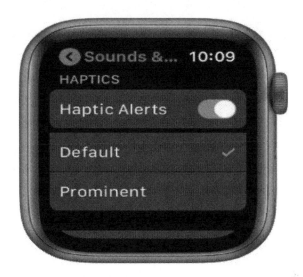

Your Apple watch also provides you with settings that let you adjust the strength of the haptics.

- Open the Settings app on your Apple Watch.
- Tap Sounds & Haptics.
- Choose Prominent Default
- Or, you can open the Apple Watch app on your iPhone, and tap My Watch
- Then tap Sounds & Haptics,

- Then choose Prominent or Default

Turn Digital Crown clicks off or on

On your Apple Watch, you will feel clicks whenever you turn the Digital Crown to scroll.

To on or off these haptics, follow these steps:

- On your Apple Watch, Open the Settings app
- Tap Sound & Haptics,
- Then turn on or off the Crown Haptics.

You can do that on your iPhone by:

- Opening the Apple Watch app.
- Then tap My Watch.
- Then tap Sounds & Haptics.

- After that, turn Crown Haptics off or on.

Chapter 43: Read News on Apple Watch

You can get updated with current events, stories, and info with the Apple Watch News app.

One of the best ways to let you view news stories are to:

- Open the News app on your Apple Watch.

- Then Tap on the News complication on a watch face.

- After that, Tap news icon on the Siri watch face.

- Then, Tap a notification from NewsTo go to the next or previous news story;

- On your Apple Watch, Open the News app

- Swipe left to read the next story if it is available.

- Swipe right to view your previous story.

- Once you scrolled to read the summary, tap Next Story located at the bottom of the screen.

- Open the News app on your Apple Watch.

- Double-click the Home button On your iPhone, to show the App Switcher.

- Then Tap the button that appears at the bottom of the screen to open News.

Chapter 44: Connect and use your AirPods With your Apple Watch

For you to use Airpods on your Apple Watch, you have to first set up your Airpods with your iPhone. Once that is done, your Airpods will automatically connect to your Apple Watch. That means, you can use any of the device with your Apple Watch.

Before you set it up, you need one of these:

- iPad, iPhone, iPod touch with iOS 10 or later
- Apple Watch with watchOS 3 or later
- Apple TV with tvOS 11 or later.

- Mac with macOS Sierra or later

If you want to use your iPhone to setup Airpods for the first time:

- On your iPhone, go to the Home screen.
- Open the case that holds your AirPods
- Hold it next to your iPhone.

- You will see a setup animation that will appear on your iPhone.
- Tap Connect,

- Then tap Done.
- Note that if you're signed into iCloud, your AirPods will automatically be set up with any of your Apple devices that you've signed in to iCloud using the same Apple ID.

Start Listening with your AirPods

Your Airpods will be **On** and ready for use immediately you take it out of the case. When they are in your ears they automatically connect to your Apple Watch and iPhone Audio at the same time.

But, to be sure that your Airpod is properly connected to your Apple Watch, take these extra steps:

- On your Apple Watch Press the digital crown to take you to the apps screen.

- Then Tap on the Settings icon.
- Next tap on Bluetooth
- Click on the AirPods under the device
- Then, see if it is connected. If it is not then connect it.

And start enjoying your Airpods and Apple Watch without taking your iPhone with you. You deserve it.

Chapter 45: Use VoiceOver on Apple Watch

VoiceOver lends some articulation to your Apple Watch when you do not casually transverse the display or you cannot even see it entirely. With simple gestures, VoiceOver cascades the interface, acting like a spokesperson reading your options aloud

1. Enable or Disable VoiceOver
2. Click the Settings icon on your Apple Watch.

To activate this function on your sync IPhone, swipe up to Accessibility > VoiceOver, and enable VoiceOver.

To turn VoiceOver off, double-tap the VoiceOver button to disable it.

"Turning VoiceOver on" or "off" are vocal instructions that enable Siri to initiate the App without your direct involvement.

As interesting as it sounds, you can enable VoiceOver on your Apple Watch with little configuration;

1. Open the Apple Watch app on your iPhone,
2. Click My Watch,
3. Proceed to Accessibility while tapping the VoiceOver option.
4. Use the Accessibility Shortcut.

Use VoiceOver for setup

VoiceOver can help you set up your Apple Watch.

On the Digital Crown display, click anywhere around it three times during setup.

Adjust VoiceOver settings

You can alter VoiceOver behaviors on Apple Watch from your iPhone.

1. Open the Apple Watch app on your iPhone,
2. Click My Watch,

Following from the two steps above, move to Accessibility and enable VoiceOver to do just this;

- Double-tap the VoiceOver button to simply deactivate the VoiceOver function.
- Apart from this, Softly haul the Speaking Rate slider to modify the speaking rate, maintaining an

285

average speech rate that is comfortable for you.

- Activate Speak on Wrist Raise to trigger a response whenever you are in motion and your wrist is fluttering about.

- Enabling Screen Curtain leaves your privacy options reduced when you put off the confidential display of your data using VoiceOver.

Tip: Screen Curtain enables your personal protection ensuring that display is left blank. To turn the display on again;

1. Open the Apple Watch app on your iPhone,

2. Go to Accessibility and click VoiceOver,

3. Tap Screen Curtain.

VoiceOver gestures

Use these gestures to control your Apple Watch with the VoiceOver function and see how much you can play around with it.

When you open gesture interface, play around the display with your fingers while also paying close attention to the audio feedback when you select a feature, swiping left and right, seeing what you can do with the voice enhancements. Doing this ensures that you explore the screen and get comfortable with gestures and accompanying sounds.

When you are through with getting comfortable with the interface and wish to return to the other features, do a finger pinch or trace a 'Z' pattern on the screen.

If you want to take further action on any function like double tap or single tap,

1. choose an app icon
2. list item
3. select the feature
4. double-click on the display options

for instance, to disable VoiceOver, select it and click twice anywhere around the window.

Most of the functions carry a single execution regardless of how much you tap it. However, some functions and features carry several actions, therefore, when you hear 'actions available', swipe to the left and right and click the display twice to initiate the instructions that you want.

When you wish to quickly do other things that will interrupt your hearing session, halt the reading session by clicking display using your fingers, when you return, resume the process with your fingers again.

Click twice with two fingers simultaneously sliding up and down to adjust VoiceOver volume.

Duplicate the same results on Apple Watch, click Apple Watch app on your IPhone and select My Watch; Swipe up to Accessibility and reduce the VoiceOver slider.

Set up Apple Watch using VoiceOver

1. Creating a VoiceOver profile on your IPhone that complements your Apple Watch where you enjoy the best of both worlds is quite practical.

2. Swipe to the right or left to select a function

3. Activate the chosen function with a stroke of your finger.

Set up Apple Watch using VoiceOver

If your Apple Watch isn't on, flip it on by pressing down the side button residing under the digital crown. You can enable this function directly on your Apple Watch by switching on VoiceOver when you click the Digital Crown three times.

To change the spoken language, tap the display until you reach your preferred language. You can create the same end results directly on your IPhone when your Apple Watch is not available.

Click Settings and move to Accessibility, enable VoiceOver on your IPhone when it is inactive by default. A very important step is to place your iPhone near your Apple Watch.

On your iPhone, select Continue, clicking it twice. Lightly stroke Set Up Apple Watch also with a double-tap.

To try automatic pairing with your IPhone and Apple Watch, point the iPhone camera at the watch, at a distance of about 6 inches away or less.

When you hear that the pairing has been confirmed, proceed to step 14. If you have any difficulty, follow steps 8 through 13 when automatic pairing is not what you want but manual connection.

Manual configuration is pretty straightforward

1. On your iPhone, select Pair Apple Watch Manually, with a double-tap.
2. On your Apple Watch, select the Info button in the bottom-right corner clicking it twice.
3. On your Apple Watch, select your Apple Watch ID near the top of the screen. You will hear the unique identifier for your Apple Watch—it's something like "Apple Watch 52345".
4. On your iPhone, select this same identifier, then double-tap.
5. Select the six-digit pairing code on your Apple Watch to hear it.

6. Enter the pairing code from your Apple Watch on your iPhone using the keyboard.

7. When pairing succeeds, you will hear "Your Apple Watch is paired." If pairing does not succeed, find out what happened by checking the alerts, allow your Apple Watch and the Apple Watch app on your iPhone return to default.

8. When pairing is complete, click anywhere on the surface of your IPhone, and select the Set Up as New Apple Watch button, and click it twice.

Choosing a wrist preference

To choose your wrist preference including the behaviors that you want to use with it,

1. click twice on the display while swinging from left to right.
2. Go over the terms and conditions, select Agree at the bottom-right, and double-tap to take you to the next prompt.
3. Select Enter Password, double-tap, and subsequently provide your Apple ID password.
4. Conclude the process by executing instructions from the audio prompts including necessary Apple Watch settings.

When your setup process has been accomplished, Apple Watch starts working in alignment with your iPhone. With just a few seconds to initialize, tap Sync Progress on your iPhone, 'Sync complete' notifies you that your Apple Watch is alive. The major indicator of this condition is obvious when the screen comes alive and then you can discover the rare gem in the features of your Apple Watch.

Apple Watch basics with VoiceOver

You can perform many functions with a press, swipe, or turning the Digital Crown. With VoiceOver on your Apple Watch, try the following while viewing the current watch face.

1. Pinch the display, swiping left and right to see the available themes.

2. Choose the one you like when you double click it. The result is a change in the watch face.

Apart from selecting a good theme for your Watch screen, you can create your own profile by swiping down to choose Customize;

1. Click it twice as you move in opposite directions to check the features.

2. Rotate the Digital Crown on the newly created features and save changes with a quick double-tap.

3. Check notifications from the watch face by swiping down with two fingers.

4. To check notifications on other screen, click the time in the top-right of the display, then swipe down with two fingers.

5. With a pinch movement of your fingers, Open Control Center from the watch face by scrolling up.

6. To access Control Center when you are using an app, click the time in the top-right of the display, then swipe up with a pinch move.

7. Press the side button to Open the Dock, rotating the Digital Crown to reach your favorite apps where you open them with two successive taps.

8. Just like what obtains on your IPhone, to open an app on your Apple Watch, long press the Digital Crown and drag down into opposite direction to select an app, click it twice and you are done.

However, Siri can also launch your apps when you long press the Digital Crown, saying 'launch' with the name of the app.

Go to the home screen to read your emails by swiping to select the app of your choice; do the same thing by asking Siri while holding down the Digital Crown, tell Siri to 'launch mail'.

You have control over apps when your finger pinches your display screen and the Digital Crown is moved to the direction where a feature you have chosen is. Pinch the display again to deselect the attribute and disable Digital Crown Navigation.

Chapter 46: Use Zoom on Apple Watch

The function of Zoom is limitless and important for a device like this.

Turn on Zoom

On your Apple Watch, click the Settings and move to Accessibility, tap Zoom and enable it.

You can replicate this setting on your Apple Watch using your IPhone directly. Click Apple Watch application on your phone, hit My Watch, click Accessibility and select Zoom.

Controlling Zoom

Once you've turned on Zoom, you can perform these actions on your Apple

Watch. Double-click on your Apple Watch display with a pinch to Zoom in or out.

Tip: Double-tap with two fingers while setting up your Apple Watch to get a better look.

To move your display focus around, you can do two things:

The first is to pinch the display with two fingers while moving it into the direction of your choice. The other option is taking a complete sweep of the whole page with Digital Crown where movement is in all directions. You can always trace your display ratio on the screen with the little Zoom button.

You can also move around the display of your Apple Watch with Digital Crown rather than using the arduous panning method all the time. Click the screen just once where the Digital Crown scrolls the breadth of your screen without using the Zoom alternative.

This is applicable when looking at details at closer pixels, like a map or a list.

You can always choose the magnifier limits that suits you when you pinch your display lens. To make this process more convenient and reduce how much magnification happens on your Apple Watch,

1. Open Apple Watch app on your IPhone
2. Click My Watch
3. Proceed to Accessibility, tap Zoom
4. Initiate the Maximum Zoom Level slider limit

Adjust text size and its weight on Apple Watch

To make text on your Apple Watch easier to read, you can display it as boldface type, and adjust the size of the text that appears in any area that supports Dynamic Type, such as the Settings.

1. Turn on grayscale
2. Open the Apple Watch app on your iPhone.
3. Tap My Watch, tap Accessibility, then turn on Grayscale.

Restarting your Apple Watch allows the change to take effect immediately.

Turn on bold text

1. Open the Settings icon on your Apple Watch.
2. Click Display & Brightness
3. Enable Bold Text.

To see changes reflected across board, restart your Apple Watch. You can also use your iPhone to activate Bold Text on your Apple Watch;

1. open the Apple Watch app on your iPhone
2. Tap My Watch,
3. go to Accessibility and enable Bold Text.

Adjust text size

1. Click Settings on your Apple Watch.
2. Hit Display & Brightness moving over to Text Size,

3. Click adjust Digital Crown to change text size.

Limit animation

Restricting the movement you see on the Home screen, including the behaviors peculiar with open apps and inactive applications are carried out with the following steps;

1. Open the Apple Watch app on your iPhone.
2. Tap My Watch,
3. Swipe up to Accessibility and Reduce Motion,
4. Enable Reduce Motion.

Tip: When you activate Reduce Motion with a grid view for the Home screen, all the app icons invariably are the same size.

Increase legibility with some backgrounds

1. Display Apple Watch app on your iPhone.
2. Tap My Watch,
3. Move to Accessibility and Reduce Transparency,
4. Enable Reduce Transparency.

On/Off button labels on Apple Watch

Activate button labels to see an extra position indicator. When button labels are on, you see a one (1) on any option that is enabled, and a zero (0) on options that are turned off.

Add labels to On/Off buttons

1. Open Settings on your Apple Watch.
2. Tap Accessibility

3. Enable On/Off Labels.

If your Apple Watch is far from you, activating labels on Apple Watch function is quite interesting on your IPhone.

1. open the Apple Watch app on your iPhone,
2. Select My Watch,
3. Click Accessibility
4. Enable On/Off Labels.

Chapter 47: Set up and use RTT on Apple Watch (cellular models only)

Real-time text (RTT) is a protocol that broadcast audio data when text is used. If you have hearing or speech difficulties, Apple Watch with cellular can communicate using RTT when you're away from your iPhone. Apple Watch uses built-in Software RTT that you configure in the Apple Watch app—it requires no additional devices.

Important: RTT is not supported by all carriers or available in all regions. When making an emergency call in the U.S.,

Apple Watch disseminate special characters or sounds that allows the operator to remain qui vive.

At the end of the day, the operator's ability to receive or respond to these timbre, varies on your location. Apple doesn't guarantee that the operator receives or responds to an RTT call.

Turn on RTT

1. Open the Apple Watch app on your iPhone.
2. Select My Watch,
3. Move to Accessibility and select RTT,
4. Enable RTT.
5. Click Relay Number and input the phone number used for relay calls using RTT.

6. Allow Send Immediately to convey each character as you type.

7. Disable to complete your messages before sending.

Start an RTT call

1. Open the Phone app on your Apple Watch.

2. Tap Contacts, then turn the Digital Crown to scroll.

3. Tap the contact you want to call, swipe up, then tap the RTT button.

4. Scribble a message, tap a reply from the list, or send an emoji.

Note: Scribble is not available in all languages.

Text appears on Apple Watch, much like a Messages conversation.

Note: A notification pops up when the recipient's device is incapable of RTT

Answer an RTT call

To receive an RTT call is pretty straightforward, more like a scene from a sci-fi movie but it is better and more convenient since you only have to raise your hand or wrist that your Apple Watch is attached to. Do the following;

1. Tap the Answer button, scroll up, then tap the RTT button.
2. Jot a message, choose a possible reply from the checklist, or click an emoji.

Note: Scribble is not available in all languages.

Edit default replies

When you make or receive an RTT call on Apple Watch, you can send a reply with just a flick of your fingers. To create extra directories of your own replies, follow these steps:

1. Open the Apple Watch app on your iPhone.
2. Tap My Watch,
3. Swipe to Accessibility and RTT,
4. Click Default Replies.
5. Tick "Add reply," enter your reply
6. Click Done.

Tip: Invariably, replies end with "GA" for go ahead, informing the recipient of the information that you are waiting for feedback.

When you have created your replies roster, you constantly add and remove some words, changing your preferences from time to time. To go about this, tick Edit in the Default Replies box.

Chapter 48: Apple Cash Payment

When you receive money in Messages, it's added to your Apple Cash card in Wallet. You can use Apple Cash right away wherever you would use Apple Pay—in stores, in apps, and on the web. And the good thing is that you can move your Apple Cash credits to your bank account.

Manage Apple Cash payment features

1. Open the Apple Watch app on your iPhone
2. Open My Watch
3. Select Wallet & Apple Pay. There you can do the following:
1. Tap the Apple Cash card to set up Apple Cash

Tip: If you already have Apple Cash set up on another device, it is instantly used on your Apple Watch without further setup.

1. Enable or disable the Apple Cash card, and the ability to send and receive money, on this device when it is provided.

See your suggested PIN

Apple Cash doesn't require a PIN since every payment is validated using a Face ID, Touch ID, and a secure passcode. In the contrary, using certain ports, requires a four-digit code prerequisite to finalize dealings.

View your Apple Cash balance

Tip: To see how much you have spent and what is left on your Apple Watch, do the following;

1. Open the Wallet app
2. Tap the Apple Cash card or double-click the side button
3. Stroke the Apple Cash card feature.

Note: Individual transaction and exchange using Apple Pay and Apple Cash are not available in all regions.

Chapter 49: Include and Utilize Passes in Wallet On Apple Watch

The Wallet app on your Apple Watch allows you to keep your boarding passes, event tickets, coupons, student ID cards, among others in one place for easy access. Passes in Wallet on your iPhone automatically sync to your Apple Watch. A pass on your Apple Watch is utilized in different ways e.g. to check in for a flight, redeem a coupon, and find your way around your personal space. Initiate the following actions to enable this function:

1. Set options for your passes

2. Click the Apple Watch app on your iPhone.

3. Swipe My Watch, then tap Wallet & Apple Pay.

4. Include a pass

Now, to add a pass, do one of the following:

Follow the instructions in the email sent to you by the pass issuer:

1. Open their app.

2. Tap Add in the notification.

3. Use a pass

Remember that you are not limited by the number of passes received from an issuer as you are likely to obtain passes from other vendors on your Apple Watch.

When you see a pass alert on your Apple Watch, follow these steps:

1. Click notification area to see the pass. Swipe up to the barcode area.
2. Provided you have a barcode privilege: Open the Wallet app on your Apple Watch, click the pass, allowing the scanner to roam over the barcode.

Use a contactless pass or student ID card

With a contactless pass or student ID card, you can use your Apple Watch to present your pass or card at a contactless reader.

If you have a contactless pass and a notification appears: swipe up to the notification panel when you have a barcode pass and a notification pops up. When there are no notifications, tap the side button twice while placing your Apple Watch some inches to the barcode reader. Ensure that the display is facing the reader to catch the signals.

Provided that your campus is supported by Apple Pay, with your student ID, stick your Apple Watch within some distance of the barcode transmitter. When your Watch vibrates, transaction is valid, and you may not use the side button function.

Rearrange passes

You exercise control on your passes no matter how much they are and regardless of the issuer of the passes. On your iPhone, take these steps:

1. open the Wallet app,
2. drag to rearrange passes.

When you are through with this process, the arrangement directly reflects on your Apple Watch.

Get a notification if your pass changes

To personalize your pass experience on your IPhone, take the following steps:

1. Open the Apple Watch app on your iPhone.

2. Tap My Watch and swipe up Wallet & Apple Pay,

3. Click **Mirror my iPhone** below notifications.

By default, your pass changes on your IPhone, simultaneously stick to your Apple Watch like a bad habit even when you activate such changes with good intentions.

Remove a pass you are done with

1. Open the Wallet app on your iPhone.

2. Hit the pass while tapping the More Info button.

3. Click Remove Pass.

The unwanted pass is therefore removed from your iPhone and Apple Watch.

Chapter 50: Start a swimming workout

The Apple Watch is designed to automatically lock the screen with a water lock for accidental taps to be avoided once a swimming workout begins. To start a swimming workout:

1. Open the Workout app.

2. Select Open Water Swim

3. Hit the digital crown and the side button simultaneously to pause or start swimming.

4. View your swimming workout summary.

5. Unlock your Apple Watch and tap End.

Note: If you decide to rest or you're done with the workout, turn the Digital Crown to get the screen unlocked and clear any water off the speaker. Once you do this, you will be prompted with sounds and get to feel the water on your wrist.

Note that Apple watches series 1 and Apple watch of the 1st generation is not suitable for swimming.

The summary that comes up on your Apple Watch displays the kind of strokes used as well as the distance you covered. The pace of each set is also made available by the "workout summary" on your iPhone.

Clear Water Manually After Swimming

Go to the bottom of the screen.

Open the Control Center by touching and holding the bottom of the screen and swiping up.

Tap the Water lock button.

Unlock the screen and clear water from the speaker by turning the Digital Crown.

Chapter 51: Using Gym Equipment with Apple Watch

The Apple Watch is designed to pair and sync data with compatible cardio equipment like elliptical, treadmills, indoor bikes and many more, thereby giving more accurate information about your workouts.

Pair your Apple Watch with gym equipment

The first step is to confirm if your equipment is compatible. You should have a message on the equipment saying "Connects with Apple Watch" or "Connect with Apple Watch."

Your watch must be configured to detect gym equipment after which you can take the following steps to pair:

1. On your Apple Watch, go to the Settings app.

2. Tap Workout.

3. Turn on Detect Gym Equipment.

Ensure your Apple watch is within a few centimeters of the contactless reader available on the gym with the display positioned facing the reader.

Once you hear a gentle tap and beep, it indicates your Apple Watch is successfully paired.

If you have your Detect Gym Equipment disabled in the Settings on your Apple watch, take the following steps:

1. Go to the Workout app.

Hold your Apple Watch near the contactless reader that is located on the gym equipment with the display positioned to face the reader.

2. Start and end a workout

3. Begin workout by pressing start on the gym equipment.

4. End workout by pressing stop on the gym equipment.

5. Once you end a workout, data from the equipment will be displayed on the workout summary which can be found in

the Activity app on your Apple watch and iPhone.

Chapter 52: Track stocks on Apple Watch

You can use the Stocks app on Apple Watches to check your stocks on your iPhone.

Ask Siri. Try: "Check yesterday's closing price for Microsoft's stock?"

To add and remove stocks:

Apart from displaying the stocks found in the Stocks app on your iPhone, you can also add and remove stocks right on your Apple Watch. Simply open the Stocks app on your Apple Watch to:

Add a stock:

1. Scroll to the bottom of the screen,

2. Then you tap Add Stock.

3. Say the name of the stock,

4. Then tap Done.

5. Then Tap the name of the stock on the list.

Remove a stock:

1.Tap the stock you want to remove

2. Firmly press the display,

3 Then tap Remove.

If you choose to reorder stocks on your Apple Watch, just open the Stocks app on your iPhone and reorder them.

Then change in order what is on your Apple Watch.

To See stock data on your Watch

1. Simply open the Stocks app on your Apple Watch.

2. Then tap a stock on the list.

3. You then tap < in the top-left corner to return to the stocks list, or just turn the Digital Crown to scroll to the next stock in the list.

To choose the data you see

1. Just open the Stocks app on your Apple Watch.

2. Firmly press the display as you view the stocks list,

3. Then tap Points, Market Cap, or Percentage.

Tip: Whenever you need to check the Stocks app on your iPhone, tap the price change for any stock to see percentage change or market cap.

To Switch to Stocks on iPhone, simply open the Stocks app on your Apple Watch.

To view the App Switcher(For iPhone X and later),

1. Double-click the Home button on your iPhone then swipe up from the bottom edge and pause to show the App Switcher.

2. Then tap the button that appears at the bottom of the screen to open Stocks.

Here's all you need to display stock information on the watch face

1. Select the stock shown on the watch face

2. Then add the Stocks complication to the watch face.

3. Then have the Apple Watch app opened on your iPhone.

4. Then tap My Watch, tap Stocks and Then choose a default stock.

Selecting the data you see on the watch face can be done if you

1. Simply open the Apple Watch app on your iPhone.

2.Tap My Watch

3. Then tap Stocks,

4 Tap any Points Change, Percentage Change, Current Price or Market Cap.

The last stock you viewed will be displayed by your Apple Watch.

Here's how you choose the data you see on the watch face

1. Simply open the Apple Watch app on your iPhone.

2. Then tap My Watch,

3.Tap Stocks,

4. Then you tap Current Price, Percentage Change, Points Change, or Market Cap.

The last stock viewed will be shown by your Apple Watch.

Chapter 53: Time Keeping Apps

To add an alarm on Apple Watch

Ask Siri. Try: "Set repeating alarm for 4 AM."

To set an alarm on Apple Watch

1. Simply open the Alarms app on your Apple Watch.

2. Then Tap Add Alarm.

3. You then Tap AM or PM,

4 Then you tap the hours or minutes. This step is unnecessary when using 24-hour time.

1. Simply adjust the Digital Crown,

2. You then tap Set.

3. To turn the alarm on or off, tap the alarm time or its switch.

This allows you to manage the repeat, label, and snooze options.

Don't Let Yourself Snooze

Whenever an alarm sounds, simply tap Snooze to wait to make the alarm sound at a later time. Here is what you do if don't want the snooze option:

1. Simply open the Alarms app on your Apple Watch.

2. Select the alarm from the list of alarms,

3. You then turn off Snooze.

To delete an alarm

1. Simply open the Alarms app on your Apple Watch.

2. Then tap the alarm on the list.

3. Then scroll to the bottom

4. Then tap Delete.

If you want to see the same alarms on both your iPhone and your Apple Watch

1. Just open the Apple Watch app on your iPhone.

2. Then tap My Watch, tap Clock,

3. Then you turn on Push Alerts from iPhone.

To set up Apple Watch as a nightstand clock with alarm

1. Have the Apple Watch app opened on your iPhone.

2. Then tap My Watch,

3. Then tap General,

4. Then turn on nightstand mode.

Connecting your Apple Watch to its charger while it is on nightstand mode causes it to display the current time and date, charging status, and the time of alarms you've set.

Tap the display or lightly nudge your Apple Watch or tap the table to check the time.

Your Apple Watch in nightstand mode will gently wake you with a unique alarm sound if you set an alarm using the Alarms app. This allows you to turn it off by pressing the side button or simply pressing the Digital Crown. Using the latter allows it to snooze for another 9 minutes.

Set a timer on Apple Watch

Do you know that you can keep track of time (up to 24hours) using the Timer app on your Apple Watch?

Ask Siri. Try: "Set a timer for 50 minutes."

To quickly set a timer

1. Just open the Timer app on your Apple Watch.

2. Then tap timer duration to start the timer.

3. Then scroll down to choose a custom time.

4. Whenever a timer goes off, tap Repeat to start a timer of the same duration.

To create a custom timer

1. Just open the Timer app on your Apple Watch.

2. Then Scroll down,

3. You then tap Custom.

4. Then tap hours, minutes, or seconds;

5. Turn the Digital Crown to adjust.

6. Then lastly, tap Start.

Your Apple Watch will find a display of the last several custom timers under Recents.

How to Time Events with a Stopwatch on Apple Watch

Apple Watches have the capacity to time full events (up to 11 hours, 55 minutes) while tracking lap or split times. After which the results are shown as a list, a graph, or live on the watches face. There is a stopwatch built in the Chronograph watch face.

To Open a stopwatch, tap the stopwatch on the watch face or simply open the Stopwatch app on your Apple Watch.

To have three watch faces showing three types of stopwatch: A digital stopwatch in the Stopwatch app, an analog stopwatch in the app, and the stopwatch control available from the Chronograph watch face.

1. Start, stop and reset the stopwatch

2. Then open the Stopwatch app on your Apple Watch,

Then do any of the following:

1. Start: Tap the green Start button.

2. Record a lap or split: Tap the white Lap button.

3. Then record the final time: Tap the red Stop button.

4. Then reset the stopwatch: Tap the white Reset button or the Lap button.

The timing should continue even if you decide to switch back to the watch face or open other apps.

You can review results on the display you used for timing and change the displays to analyze your lap times and fastest/slowest laps (marked with green and red) in your preferred format. If the display includes a list of lap times, you can then turn the Digital Crown to scroll.

How to change the stopwatch format

1. Simply open the Stopwatch app on your Apple Watch.

2. Then firmly press the display,

3. You could then tap any of Hybrid, Analog, Digital or Graph.

Here's how you switch between 1 dial and 3 dials with splits if you choose Analog.

1. To view separate minute, second, and tenths dials above a scrolling list of lap

times simply tap the 1-dial analog stopwatch.

2. Then tap the watch face again to return to the 1-dial analog stopwatch.

To check the time in other locations using World Clock on Apple Watch

Ask Siri. **Try: "What time is it in London?"**

To add and remove cities in World Clock

1. Just open the World Clock app on your Apple Watch.

2. Then tap Add City.

3. Then tap Dictation or Scribble,

4. You then enter the city name.

You should note that Scribble is not available in all languages.

Then tap the city name to add it to World Clock.

To remove a city, simply swipe left on its name, then tap X. Firmly press the display then tap Remove to remove a city when viewing its info.

The cities added on your iPhone will also appear in World Clock on your Apple Watch.

To check the time in another city

1. Simply open the World Clock app on your Apple Watch.

2. Swipe the screen or turn the Digital Crown to scroll the list.

Tap the city on the list to see more information about a city, including the time of sunrise and sunset.You can also scroll to see the next city on your list while you're viewing info about a city.

Then swipe right to return to the city list or tap < in the top-left corner when you are done.

If you would love to constantly check any city's time, just add the world clock to your watch face and choose a city to display.

Change city abbreviations

Follow these steps to change city abbreviations used on your Apple Watch:

1. Have the Apple Watch app opened on your iPhone

2. Then tap My Watch,

3. Then go to Clock > City Abbreviations.

4. Lastly, tap any city to change its abbreviation.

Chapter 54: The Best Way to Sell, Protect Or Gift Away an Apple Watch

Make sure you un-pair your Apple Watch before you sell or gift it out. This way, you can erase its contents, remove Activation Lock and keep yourself safe. You could put your Apple Watch in lost mode if you lose it.

How you un-pair your Apple Watch and remove the Activation Lock

1. Just open the Apple Watch app on your iPhone.

2. Then tap My Watch,

3. You then tap your Apple Watch at the top of the screen.

4. Then tap the Info button,

5. Then lastly tap Unpair Apple Watch.

The steps above ensure that your Apple Watch is erased and removed from your iCloud account, and the Activation Lock is removed.

How to Locate Your Apple Watch

1.Open the Apple Watch app on your iPhone.

2. Then tap My Watch,

3. You then tap your Apple Watch at the top of the screen.

4. Tap the Info button,

5. After which you then tap Find My Apple Watch.

6. When you get there, tap your watch to see its location on a map.

The next thing is to tap Play Sound if your Apple Watch is at your location(as revealed by the map).

Chapter 55: Mark Your Apple Watch as Lost

Your Apple Watch is locked with a passcode when you mark it as lost. This prevents others from accessing delicate information while suspending the ability to make payments with Apple Pay using credit or debit cards in Wallet.

1. Just open the Apple Watch app on your iPhone.

2. Tap My Watch,

3. You then tap your Apple Watch at the top of the screen.

4. Next, you tap the Info button,

5. Then you tap Find My Apple Watch.

6. Tap Activate under Mark As Lost when you get there(in 5 above).

7. To display a message that includes a contact number, and a message indicating the Apple Watch is lost, Tap **Enable** to mark Apple Watch as lost.

When you find your Apple Watch, you can either enter your passcode on the watch or go to your iPhone:

1.Open Find My,

2. Tap Devices,

3. Tap your Apple Watch,

4. Tap Activated,

5. Lastly, tap Turn Off Mark As Lost.

How to Erase A Lost Apple Watch

Before erasing your device, try to locate it or play a sound on it because after erasing it, you won't be able to use Find My to do either.

1. Just open the Apple Watch app on your iPhone.

2. First, tap My Watch,

3. You then tap your Apple Watch at the top of the screen.

4. Then tap the Info button,

5. You then tap Find My Apple Watch.

Go to Find My app on your iPhone,

1. Tap your watch,

2. You then tap Erase This Device.

To remove payment cards using a web browser

Sign in to appleid.apple.com using your Apple ID to remove your cards in an event where your Apple Watch could lost or stolen

Choose the device in the Device area. Then,

Simply click Remove All under Apple Pay.

In the event that your iPhone and Apple Watch are no longer connected, or say one of them isn't functioning well, you can change this by

1.Erasing the contents of your Apple Watch first after which

2. You then unpair it using the Apple Watch app on your iPhone (if available).

How To See information about Apple Watch

On your Apple Watch,

1. Just open the Settings app,

2. Then go to General

3.Go to **About. And** you will find the following items:

- Name
- Network
- Number of songs, photos, and apps
- Capacity and available storage space
- Software version
- Carrier—Apple Watch with cellular only

- Model number
- ICCID, IMEI, MEID, EID and modem firmware—Apple Watch with cellular only
- Serial number
- MAC and Bluetooth addresses
- SEID
- Legal Info

To view regulatory marks,

1. Open Settings,

2. You then go to General > Regulatory.

You also get to view this information on the paired iPhone

1.Have the Apple Watch app opened on your iPhone,

2. Then tap My Watch,

3. You then go to General > About.

4. You then scroll to the bottom and tap Legal to view Legal Notices, License, information on where to find the Warranty, and RF Exposure information.

Chapter 56: Other Included Tips and Tricks to keep in mind

Here are some key tips to keep in mind when using your Apple Watch Series 5

How to Take Screenshot on Apple Watch

One of the perks of using the Apple Watch is that it can allow you to take screenshots.

But since its latest update, Apple has disabled the ability for you to take a screenshot by default.

To enable screenshots:

• Tap on Apple Watch app on your iPhone.

- Swipe down to General and scroll to the bottom.

- A toggle will appear for you to Enable Screenshots. Turn it on. With this, you have enabled screenshot on Apple Watch.

- To take screenshots, press the Digital Crown and the Side button at the same time.

Note that, if you toggle **Disable Screenshots** or **turn off screenshots,** pressing the Digital Crown and Side button at the same time will become inactive.

Customize Control Center

In watchOS 6, you can customize the Control Center layout to suit your needs. Just scroll to the bottom of the Control Center and tap on the Edit button

There are times when you don't want your Apple Watch to light up every time you move your hand or when you get a call or notification. Swipe up to access Control Center and tap on the Cinema Mode (or Theater mode) icon to enable it.

Use the Flashlight

Apple Watch features a built-in flashlight. To access it, Swipe up to reveal Control Center and tap on the Flashlight icon.

You can also swipe between multiple modes like flashing white, plain white and emergency red.

How to Mute Apple Watch

By default, your apple watch makes a sound whenever you get a notification.

But you can mute stop the amount of noise it makes.

To do this:

- Swipe up to reveal the Control Center

- Then you can to tap on the Bell icon to enable Silent mode.

- And that is it.

Mono Audio and Audio Balance On Apple Watch

If you prefer listening to ambidextrous audio signals from both audio channels on speakers or headphones connected to your Apple Watch, turn on Mono Audio. You can also adjust the left-right balance of your Apple Watch audio, using stereo or mono capacities.

Change Audio Settings

When you click the Apple Watch app on your iPhone device, hit My Watch, and swipe down to Accessibility where you take the following actions;

1. Enable Mono Audio when you swap stereo to mono audio.
2. Increase or decrease audio balance by dragging down the digital slider at intervals just below Mono Audio.

The Accessibility Shortcut on Apple Watch

For your convenience and easy access to your favorite apps, with a rapid triple-tap, allow your Digital Crown to enable VoiceOver or disable Zoom.

Set the Accessibility Shortcut

1. Click the Apple Watch app on your iPhone.

2. Tap My Watch, go to Accessibility > Accessibility Shortcut,

3. Select VoiceOver or Zoom.

Use the shortcut

To see your changed settings, hit the Digital Crown three times in quick succession. Click through three times again to disable accessibility feature on the Digital Crown.

Set the side button speed

1. Activate the Apple Watch app on your iPhone.

2. Tap My Watch and swipe down to Accessibility,

3. Click Side Button Click Speed, choosing a speed that is convenient.

Troubleshooting Tips

Restart Apple Watch

Here's how to restart your Apple Watch and its paired iPhone when your device has issues:

1. Turn off your Apple Watch

2. Press and hold the side button until the sliders appear,

3. You then drag the Power Off slider to the right. You can turn on your Apple Watch by holding down the side button until the Apple logo appears.

Caveat: Your Apple Watch can't be restarted while it's charging.

To restart the paired iPhone

1. Turn off your iPhone: If your model has Face ID

2. Press and hold the side button and a volume button,

3. Then drag the slider to the right. Models without Face ID can be turned off by pressing and holding the side or top button until the slider appears, after which the slider is dragged to the right. All models are turned off by simply going to Settings > General > Shut Down.

Whenever you want to turn on your iPhone, press down the side or top button until the Apple logo appears.

How to Force Apple Watch to restart

It's best to only force restart your Apple Watch when you can't restart it or when you have issues with it.

Force restart it by holding down the side button and the Digital Crown at the same time until the Apple logo appears (say ten seconds).

To Erase Apple Watch

1. Just open the Settings app on your Apple Watch.

2. Then go to General > Reset, tap Erase All Content and Settings,

3. You then enter your passcode.

You are offered two options if your Apple Watch has a cellular plan:

Completely   erasing   your   Apple
Watch,(choose Erase All).

OR

Erasing and then restoring it with your
cellular plan is in place (choose Erase All &
Keep Plan).

Another option is to:

1. Have the Apple Watch app opened on
your iPhone

2. Tap My Watch,

3. Go to General > Reset

4. Then tap Erase Apple Watch Content
and Settings.

If accessing the Settings app on your
Apple Watch is difficult because you've
forgotten your passcode:

1. Put your Apple Watch on its charger

2. Then press and hold the side button until you see Power Off.

3. Then firmly press the Power Off slider,

4. Then you lift your finger.

5. After which you tap Erase all content and settings.

Once your Apple Watch restarts, you will need to re-pair your Apple Watch with your iPhone:

1. Start by opening the Apple Watch app on your iPhone,

2..Then you follow the instructions shown on your iPhone and Apple Watch.

How to remove your cellular plan

1. Simply open the Apple Watch app on your iPhone.

2. Then tap My Watch,

3.Tap Cellular,

4. You then tap the Info button next to your cellular plan.

5. Next, tap Remove [name of carrier] Plan,

6. Then you confirm your choice.

Try contacting your carrier to remove your Apple Watch from your cellular plan.

How to restore Apple Watch from a backup

Did you know that your Apple Watch is backed up automatically to your paired iPhone and that you could restore it from a stored backup? The Apple Watch backups are included in your backups to your iPhone: to Mac, iCloud, or PC.Note that those backups not made on iCloud, can't be viewed.

How To Back up and Restore Apple Watch

Back up your Apple Watch: The Apple Watch content is backed up continuously to the iPhone it is paired with. A backup is performed first if you choose to un-pair the devices.

Restore your Apple Watch from a backup: You could choose Restore from Backup to select a stored backup whenever you want to pair your Apple Watch with the same iPhone, or you just get yourself a new Apple Watch.

If you're having issues connecting your Bluetooth accessory because it won't connect, then follow these processes:

1. See if the Airplane Mode of your Watch face is ON.

2. If it is ON, type Settings > Airplane Mode, then turn it off.

3. Ensure your accessory is powered on and it is fully charged.

4. If you notice that the accessory is in the Settings and on the Bluetooth on your

Apple Watch, but you still can't connect it, use the steps above to unpair the accessory.

5. Then Try to pair the accessory again.

How To Update Apple Watch software

Checking for Apple Watch updates allows you to update its software to the latest version. Here's how to do that:

1. Check for and install software updates

Open the Apple Watch app on your iPhone.

2. Tap My Watch,

3. Go to General > Software Update,

4. Then, if an update is available,

5. You then tap Download and Install.

Conclusion

We do hope you have learnt a great deal from this guide. If you have, please leave a review on Amazon.

Thanks a lot.

Best Regards,

Nelson Newman

Other books by the Author

1. <u>iPad Pro Guide: The Ultimate & Complete 2019 Beginners Manual to Learn All about the new iPadOS Update in the iPad and iPad Pro</u>

Index

Z

Made in the USA
San Bernardino, CA
31 October 2019